50 WAYS TO PRAY

50 WAYS TO PRAY

Practices from Many Traditions and Times

TERESA A. BLYTHE

ABINGDON PRESS
Nashville

50 WAYS TO PRAY
PRACTICES FROM MANY TRADITIONS AND TIMES

Copyright © 2006 by Abingdon Press

This book is printed on acid-free paper.

Library of Congress Cataloging in Publication Data

Blythe, Teresa.
  50 ways to pray : practices from many traditions and times / Teresa A. Blythe.
      p. cm.
  ISBN 0-687-33104-8 (binding: adhesive perfect : alk. paper)
  1. Prayer—Christianity. I. Title.

BV215.B57 2006
248.3'2—dc22

2005030936

ISBN 13: 978-0-687-33104-8

12 13 14 15 – 10 9 8

MANUFACTURED IN THE UNITED STATES OF AMERICA

To my husband Duane Schneider,
for his encouragement,
support, and prayers

CONTENTS

PREFACE

A S JESUS' disciples begged him to teach them to pray, we too long for instruction in prayer, contemplation, meditation, and discernment—teachers and resources inviting us into a living relationship with God. The explosion of interest today in Christian mystics, ancient prayer practices, and guided meditations speaks to a need for more hands-on tools that will help us pray in traditional as well as new and ever-exciting ways. This book is intended to address that need.

Like many Protestant Christians, I grew up thinking there was only one way to pray—speaking either silently or out loud to God, asking for what I and the world needed; thanking God for all good things; and asking that God's will be done. In worship these prayers were usually said by professional clergy at the front of the sanctuary. There were a few common prayers recited, such as the Lord's Prayer and a variety of prayers of confession, but that was about the extent of it. It was as though churches had "outsourced" public (and in some cases private) prayer to professionals. Mystical experiences, silent encounters, and guided meditations were *not* considered to be prayer and were, in fact, looked on with suspicion.

It wasn't until I met a spiritual director in the late 1980s that I was invited to pray in new and different ways. Encountering the Holy through prayer practices that Christian mystics and many devout Catholics had been using for centuries was pivotal to my spiritual development. My image of God was transformed and the course of my life's journey changed significantly. I enrolled in San Francisco Theological Seminary's Master of Divinity and Diploma in the Art of Spiritual Direction programs and became a spiritual director.

In seminary, I collected hundreds of classroom handouts and notes from reading assignments that became for me an assortment of prayer "helps" and exercises kept in a fat purple binder. Many times, after sharing the contents of this notebook with friends and prayer groups, I have been asked to print the exercises for people to use at home, with small groups, or in worship. One astute friend, talking with me about my next writing project in Christian spirituality, pointed to the purple binder and said, *"That's* your next book!"

And so it is.

These exercises, courtesy of the communion of saints who have gone before (and a few still on earth), invite us into new ways of walking with God. They are ways to become in tune with God's Spirit, which is already moving in our lives, one or more steps ahead of us, desiring to live as our eternal flame. They help us as individuals and groups to reclaim our power to be in relationship with God in innumerable ways.

Each of the exercises includes not only instructions on how to use it as a prayer practice, but also some background, an introduction, a statement of intention, and tips to help you become comfortable with the practice. For those of you wanting to lead these practices in a group, there are special instructions and information in the Leader's Guide at the end of the book.

It is my hope that this book will provide at least fifty ways you may take steps in a lifelong walk with God. It is written for you, the seeker and sojourner, as well as you, the church leader, youth minister, retreat facilitator, or worship planner.

It is for all of us who thought we only knew one way to pray.

INTRODUCTION

Y OU'VE FELT the call. Perhaps, through prayer, God is prompting you to be more intentional about drawing near to the Source of Life. Maybe you've grown a little tired of the tried and true devotional methods of your past and wonder just how a person moves deeper in awareness and understanding of the presence of God. I'm a big believer in variety. Once I experienced a variety of ways to pray and listen to the Spirit, I began to get to know God, enjoy God, and be at peace with God's creation a whole lot more.

So, appreciate the variety of activities presented in this book. Don't expect every one to lead you to mystical and soul-expanding union with God. Even the most mature Christians will tell you that such an experience is rare and providential—it is not the goal. To enjoy and live in the light of God is the goal, and that is usually experienced in daily, ordinary life.

Also, do not approach these prayer activities as a way of currying divine favor. This is not a handbook for "extreme spirituality" nor do you get "heavenly points" for adding new prayer practices to your life. Do not pray out of fear, obligation, or competition. Pray out of gratitude and desire, remembering that God loves a *cheerful* giver (2 Corinthians 9:7).

As you pray in different ways, be open to surprising, even subtle shifts in awareness. You may find a few practices listed here to be ones you want to spend a long time with. That's great. Sticking with a practice through thick and thin is a wonderful way to grow closer to God. Many people practice a form of *lectio divina* (chapter 3) or the Ignatian Examen (chapter 4) every day.

Also, be aware that mining the depths of our souls can be tough work at times. We discover we are in need of healing, and recovery almost always involves some pain. If we are honest in our prayers and conversations with God, we come face to face with ugly emotions, destructive habits, and self-deception. I remember once turning to prayer after a serious illness and beginning to sob in distress. Concerned about this, I consulted my pastor, asking, "Isn't prayer supposed to make me feel better?" She smiled and said, "Not all the time. Prayer opens our heart to the loving presence of God, and that presence may ask us to grieve and let ourselves experience our pain." That's when I stopped seeing prayer as a remedy and allowed it to become a living relationship with the living God.

Begin this adventure with an open mind and heart. Know that it will, at times, delight you and, at other times, invite you to face up to your fears, inadequacies, and lack of faith. If the road of spiritual practice produces anxiety or a feeling of being in too deep, don't despair or stop praying. Consult with a trusted, spiritually mature friend, a pastor, or a spiritual director about what you are experiencing. Spiritual directors, in particular, are trained to assist you in discovering where God may be leading you in these prayer experiences. They also can help you discern which practices are the most helpful for you at this time in your life. To find a spiritual director, consult any Christian retreat center in your area, or contact Spiritual Directors International (information at www.sdiworld.org) and ask where to begin.

Chapter 1

BIBLICAL REFLECTIONS

THE BIBLE is a wonderful starting point for exploring Christian spirituality. Though you may be familiar with a scholarly approach to the Bible, these exercises will not be academic in nature. They are more about ruminating and mining Scripture for wisdom that applies to our inner being than they are about digging in the history, context, and authorship—all meaningful pursuits in Bible study. Many of the exercises here focus on a question posed by Jesus or by the story itself and how we might answer it after much consideration and prayer.

The challenge in reflecting on the Bible is that the Bible is so many things to so many people. For some Christians, it is the inerrant word of God given to humanity directly by God to instruct us in salvation. For others, it is not the *last word* about God's love of creation, but rather the start of a centuries-long dialogue between humans and the Creator. For our purposes, the Bible will be a tool for digging deeper into our souls for faith development—not primarily a guidebook or outside authority.

Our approach to Scriptures in this chapter is very much in keeping with the way Scriptures have been read by the faithful for eons—as a love letter with many important questions we want to ponder together.

Meditation on the Heart's Longing

Jesus was famous for asking important questions. The questions of Jesus are an excellent starting place for spiritual practice. I have used variations of this exercise alone, in retreats, and in individual spiritual direction sessions to help people focus on the longing of their hearts. Hearing the words from Jesus legitimizes the question for many devout Christians. This exercise may be revisited time and time again, because invariably our heart's longings change as our journeys evolve.

Intention

Responding to the voice of Jesus as he asks, "What are you looking for?"

The Exercise

- Start with a period of silence. Pray for the Spirit's guidance in discovering your heart's deepest desire.
- Read John 1:35-38 slowly once.

  The next day John again was standing with two of his disciples, and as he watched Jesus walk by, he exclaimed, "Look, here is the Lamb of God!" The two disciples heard him say this, and they followed Jesus. When Jesus turned and saw them following, he said to them, "What are you looking for?"

- Allow two minutes of silence.
- Read the passage again, slowly.
- Allow two minutes of silence.
- Consider: What are you looking for this day? If Jesus were to ask you this question, what would you say? What are you searching for? What are you longing for?
- Spend about ten minutes in silence considering the question. Write an answer.
- End your reflection by noticing where you felt particularly close to God or Jesus in this exercise. Where did you feel a sense of God's Spirit? Where did you feel the Spirit blocked? What contributed to freedom of the Spirit? What contributed to blocks of the Spirit?

Tip

A contemplative and calm pace will help you enter the Scripture passage more fully. Don't rush the meditation. If you find your mind wandering from the question to issues of biblical history or interpretation, gently return to the question at hand. Notice the places where you felt most at peace in the meditation. Also notice any places where you felt discomfort. Offer all those places to God's care as you end this reflection.

Dialoguing with Scripture

Scripture doesn't have to be one-way communication. It invites us to respond, question, debate, and celebrate its offering. When we begin to "talk back" to Scripture, it comes alive and becomes interactive. Our critical thinking skills engage with our spiritual "feelers," strengthening our faith.

Intention

A deepening of faith as we connect intellectually and spiritually with a figure in Scripture.

The Exercise

- Choose one of the following Scriptures for reflection:
    Exodus 1:8-22—The Hebrew midwives fear God
    Exodus 18:13-27—Jethro's advice to Moses
    1 Samuel 3—The call of Samuel
    Mark 9:14-29—Jesus heals the afflicted boy
    Luke 8:22-25—Jesus calms a storm
    Luke 10:25-37—The Good Samaritan
    Luke 10:38-42—Jesus visits Martha and Mary
    Luke 19:1-10—Jesus and Zacchaeus

- Read the selected Scripture slowly. You may want to read it more than once.
- Consider which character in the story you would like to interact with. It could be a person you find agreeable, or a person you want to question or debate with. Who are you drawn to? When you decide on a character, write the name at the top of your paper.
- Hold an imaginary conversation—on paper—with the character in the story. You may want to stick with the theme of the Scripture and talk about that, or you may want to discuss other topics. It is completely up to you. Let your imagination roll free and see what transpires. (20 minutes)
- When you are finished, read your dialogue aloud.
- What is it like to have a conversation with a biblical figure? Why did you choose the character you chose? Did anything in the conversation surprise you? Did anything in the conversation move you? Did you feel any inner blocks to doing this sort of exercise? Did you feel the presence and guidance of God in the dialogue? What did you learn about yourself as you engaged this biblical figure? How easy or difficult is it for you to have these kinds of imaginary conversations? How useful would you say such conversations are for you?
- End your reflection time with a prayer of gratitude for what you experienced.

Tip

You don't have to be an excellent writer to enjoy this exercise. No one but you has to read what you've written. Just write from the heart and imagination.

Listening to Wisdom

Biblical Wisdom literature is rich soil for spiritual gardening. The beauty of this genre is that it is almost entirely devoted to describing the human being's experience of God—something the seeker in us can relate to. What you don't find in Wisdom literature is a lot of talk about salvation. The writers were more interested in providing instructions for how to live along the way.

Jesus would have been very familiar with the images and philosophies that appear in Wisdom literature. So, it is not surprising that the two passages chosen for reflection in this exercise have historical connections.

Intention

Linking God's wisdom to our own.

The Exercise

- Sirach 6:18-19, 24-28 (found in the Apocryphal-Deuterocanonical portion of the Bibles used by Orthodox and Catholic churches)

Blessings of Wisdom
My child, from your youth choose discipline,
    and when you have gray hair you will still find wisdom.
Come to her like one who plows and sows,
    and wait for her good harvest.
For when you cultivate her you will toil but little,
    and soon you will eat of her produce. . . .
Put your feet into her fetters,
    and your neck into her collar.
Bend your shoulders and carry her,
    and do not fret under her bonds.
Come to her with all your soul,
    and keep her ways with all your might.
Search out and seek, and she will become known to you;
    and when you get hold of her, do not let her go.
For at last you will find the rest she gives,
    and she will be changed into joy for you.

- Read Matthew 11: 28-30:

    Come to me, all you that are weary and are carrying heavy burdens, and I will give you rest. Take my yoke upon you, and learn from me; for I am gentle and humble in heart, and you will find rest for your souls. For my yoke is easy, and my burden is light.

- Spend the next ten minutes silently reading each passage slowly and carefully, *looking for a word of instruction for your life.* What do you hear or read that seems to be speaking just to you right now? Write down your word or words of instruction.
- Now reflect even more deeply on the word or words of instruction. How exactly might you live out the instruction this week? Write down your thoughts on the action that it prompts.
- Of the two passages you read, which did you find most meaningful? Why? What was it like to reflect on a word or words of instruction? Do you generally respond well to receiving instruction from others? What is it like to receive instruction from God or God's word? Was any part of this exercise difficult for you? Did you feel a resistance to any part of it? If so, can you name the resistance? In what way is reflecting on Wisdom literature different from reflecting on a parable of Jesus? Or a gospel narrative?
- End with a prayer of gratitude to God for the gift of God's wisdom to us.

Tip

Some background research on the book of Sirach and other biblical Wisdom literature might be helpful in getting the most from this exercise. *Harper's Bible Dictionary* (1996) and the *New Interpreter's Study Bible* (2003) are both excellent resources. Also, you can find the Sirach scripture online at the Christian Classics Ethereal Library of Calvin College at www.ccel.org.

What Do You Want from God?

Spiritual director and retreat leader Kay Collette of San Rafael, California, uses this guided meditation to help people get in touch with their feelings about God and what they desire from God. She teaches that our deepest desires are keys to knowing our self and God. Many of us are used to feeling that God has expectations of us, but feel somehow ashamed that we have expectations of God. This Scripture passage invites us to share those expectations openly.

This exercise is a Scripture reflection much like ones St. Ignatius—sixteenth century founder of the Jesuit Order and author—suggests in his Spiritual Exercises. Ignatian spirituality, with its emphasis on finding God in our ordinary, daily lives, will be explored in many upcoming exercises as well.

Intention

Becoming deeply honest with God about our desires.

The Exercise

• Read Mark 10:35-40 through twice, slowly.

> *James and John, the sons of Zebedee, came forward to him and said to him, "Teacher, we want you to do for us whatever we ask of you." And he said to them, "What is it you want me to do for you?" And they said to him, "Grant us to sit, one at your right hand and one at your left, in your glory." But Jesus said to them, "You do not know what you are asking. Are you able to drink the cup that I drink, or be baptized with the baptism that I am baptized with?" They replied, "We are able." Then Jesus said to them, "The cup that I drink you will drink; and with the baptism with which I am baptized, you will be baptized; but to sit at my right hand or at my left is not mine to grant, but it is for those for whom it has been prepared."*

• After reading, make yourself comfortable and prepare for an imaginative journey. You may write your responses to the questions in the guided meditation.
• Now, keeping the Mark 10 passage close by, slowly read the following guided meditation, stopping at the end of every sentence to let your imagination roll.
• Imagine that you are in the company of James, John, and Jesus. Notice the surroundings. What does the setting look like? What time of day is it? What is the temperature? Imagine, feel, and—in your mind's eye—enter the scene.
• Now James and John make their request of Jesus: "Teacher, we want you to do for us whatever we ask of you." What is your reaction? What do you want to say to James and John? What do you want to say to Jesus? Notice how everyone in the scene

is relating to one another. Has anything about the setting changed? Stay rooted in the scene.

- Listen as Jesus responds: "What is it you want me to do for you?"
- For a moment, let James and John's reply about sitting in glory at the right and left hand of Jesus, fade into the background. Imagine that Jesus is asking you the question.
- "What is it you want me to do for you?" How do you answer?
- "What is it you want me to do for you?" What is your most honest reply?
- "What is it you want me to do for you?"
- Now that you have answered Jesus' question, what response do you hear from Jesus to your request?
- Open up the conversation to include James, John, Jesus, and yourself. Other people may have joined in, which is fine. Listen to what each person in the conversation has to say.
- Now it's time to wrap up this conversation. Silently speak to each person, expressing your appreciation for what they had to offer. Say a special thanks to Jesus for asking the question.
- Now slowly and gently bring your attention to the present.

Step outside the imaginative prayer and reflect upon what it was like to pray with your imagination. What physical setting did you "see" in your mind's eye? What did you say to James and John after their initial statement to Jesus? What response did you have to Jesus' question? Did the response change during the repeating of the question and the silence? What did any of the other characters say in response to your request? Did any figures other than James, John, and Jesus show up for you? Did the imaginative reflection take any unexpected twists or turns? Did you feel any reluctance to praying in this way? If so, what were you feeling? Did the prayer time make the discomfort fade or become stronger?

End with a few words of gratitude for this experience.

Tip

If you find it hard to read the guided mediation and visualize at the same time, then read the guided meditation portion into a tape recorder so you can play it back and follow along unencumbered by reading.

Stages of the Journey

Like the children of Israel after the exodus, we are all on a wilderness journey that we trust is leading to the promised land. In this exercise, we reflect on what stage of the journey we are presently in. Are we trekking along the arduous route in the wilderness? Are we resting at the way station of Mount Horeb? Or are we making that risky but hope-filled march into the promised land? It is important to note not only where we are on the journey, but also where we long to be.

The people of Israel were especially fond of Mount Horeb (also known as Mount Sinai) because it was where Moses received important revelation from God. Still, the people were in a holding pattern—no longer in Egypt and not yet in their promised land.

No stage of the journey is less important than another. What is important is listening to the voice of God, as Moses did when he heard God say, "You have stayed long enough at this mountain."

Intention

Remembering the stages of our spiritual journey and observing how God interacts with us along the journey.

The Exercise

• Read Deuteronomy 1:6-8 twice, slowly:

The LORD our God spoke to us at Horeb, saying, "You have stayed long enough at this mountain. Resume your journey, and go into the hill country of the Amorites as well as into the neighboring regions—

the Arabah, the hill country, the Shephelah, the Negeb, and the sea-coast—the land of the Canaanites and the Lebanon, as far as the great river, the river Euphrates. See, I have set the land before you; go in and take possession of the land that I swore to your ancestors, to Abraham, to Isaac, and to Jacob, to give to them and to their descendants after them."

- On a sheet of paper, in any form you choose, create a timeline of your own spiritual journey, considering the various stages of the people of Israel's journey:

  The Egypt stage. Think about a pivotal point in your life, a time when you needed some kind of deliverance. It does not necessarily have to be a time of great oppression or hardship, but it could be. What was *your* Egypt? Somewhere on your page, make a note or an image indicating an Egypt stage.

  The Wilderness stage. Now think about the time that followed the exit from your Egypt. Did it involve wandering or seeking? Were there some stops along the way? Some highlights or lowlights? Spend a few minutes thinking about a wilderness stage in your life. If it helps, draw a line from Egypt (doesn't have to be straight!) to indicate the wilderness trek.

  The Mount Horeb stage. Along your life's journey, was there a time of revelation for you? A resting place? An event for which you have fond memories? Make a note or an image indicating your Mount Horeb stage. Is it connected to the wilderness trek? If so, connect your line to your Mount Horeb.

Stay at your symbolic Mount Horeb for a few minutes in silence. As you reflect on Mount Horeb, can you remember a time when you felt God indicating it was time to move on? Remember what it felt like for God to say something like, "You have stayed long enough at this mountain. Resume your journey and go into the promised land." If you cannot think of an experience like that, imagine what it might have felt like for the people of Israel to hear God say that to them. You may want to write a few words about that feeling.

The Promised Land. Now, somewhere on your page, make a note or image indicating the promised land. What is that for you? What has God promised to you? What do you need to move toward? If you feel you have arrived at the promised land, think about any connections between your Mount Horeb experiences and where you ended up. Was it hard to move from Mount Horeb to the promised land? If you have no idea what the promised land is for you, think about how the people of Israel may have felt when God told them to take possession of the land set before them.

- Bring your attention now to the present. Which stage do you feel you've spent the most time in?
- Which stage are you in now? Is the metaphor of journey meaningful? Why or why not? What stage of the Israelites' journey do you find most interesting or helpful for your life? What, if anything, about the passage meant the most to you? What, if anything, about the passage disturbed you?
- End your reflection by writing a word or two of gratitude to God for the journey you are on.

Tips

Keep a journal or notebook handy for activities, like this one, that include writing or drawing.

If you have a hard time identifying times in your life when you felt guided by God, consider all the important events and changes in your life, including places where you felt intensely loved and nurtured by others.

The Drama of Martha and Mary

It's hard *not* to relate to the story of Jesus visiting Martha and Mary. The story is so dramatic, and most of us find some aspect of ourselves in the story. That's why retelling and embodying the story in dramatic presentation opens it up to us in new ways.

Intention

A deeper understanding of what "the better part" of life with Jesus is for us.

The Exercise

Read through the following passage twice, slowly.

> Now as they went on their way, he entered a certain village, where a woman named Martha welcomed him into her home. She had a sister named Mary, who sat at the Lord's feet and listened to what he was saying. But Martha was distracted by her many tasks; so she came to him and asked, "Lord, do you not care that my sister has left me to do all the work by myself? Tell her then to help me." But the Lord answered her, "Martha, Martha, you are worried and distracted by many things; there is need of only one thing. Mary has chosen the better part, which will not be taken away from her." (Luke 10:38-42)

- Write a short, casual drama—no more than five minutes long—that retains the *meaning* of the story as you understand it but updates it for our time. Feel free to change the situation, the characters, and even the gender. If you like, write your drama in dialogue form using narration.
- Now read your drama aloud, imagining the characters coming to life as you read their words.
- Reflect on your drama. What came alive for you in the retelling of this gospel story? What, if anything, seemed new or different in the retelling? What moved you most? What changes did you make to tell this story in a way that has meaning today? Do you identify with the same character as you did in previous readings? Which character do you *want* to identify with? Why? Who in our popular culture today seems to be more like Martha? Who in our popular culture today seems to be more like Mary? In what situations do you find yourself assuming a Martha attitude? In what situations do you find yourself assuming a Mary attitude? What do you think "the better part" might be for your life?
- End your creative adaptation of Scripture with a few moments of silence.

Tips

This is a familiar passage for many people. Try to put aside preconceived notions about the passage and look at this story like a fine, multifaceted jewel, considering the many ways it reflects the light.

For some, this is a troubling passage. It seems as though Jesus is failing to acknowledge the amount of work and care that goes into preparing a home to receive guests. Most biblical scholars today urge us to look at the core of what Jesus was saying to Martha and Mary. It is not that housework is not important or holy; it is more that our distractions and anxious natures keep us from what is truly holy.

Create Your Own Psalm

The psalms are among the most human expressions found in the Bible. Some of them are so raw we want to look away—and, in fact, many of our lectionary texts skip over passages filled with rage and violence. But the psalms give us confidence that no matter what emotion we are feeling, we can share it with God.

In this exercise, you will be asked to think about your deepest longing before God and write your own psalm. It doesn't matter whether you think of yourself as a writer or not. This is heartfelt communication, not an exercise in pretty writing.

Before you write your psalm, read a few of the psalms in the Bible—ones that express what you are feeling—and listen to their passion. You may even choose to rewrite one of them instead of creating your own from scratch.

Intention

To be Psalmists and express ourselves to God.

The Exercise

- Find a comfortable desk or table to write on. Gather writing materials and a Bible.
- Ask God's Spirit to enliven you as you search the psalms and create your own.
- First, identify what you would like to express to God. What is your deepest longing right now? What is your truest feeling? Based on what you are feeling, read a related psalm from the Bible.

  Joy—Psalm 11, 18, 23, 27, 33, 84, 87, 103, 112, 122, 150
  Peace—Psalm 23, 63, 103
  Love—Psalm 33, 62, 99, 103, 104, 139, 145
  Gratitude—Psalm 30, 32, 65, 75, 77, 103, 118, 136
  Fear—Psalm 86, 130, 131
  Anger or rage—Psalm 55, 58, 94
  Persecution—Psalm 17, 26, 35, 69, 141
  Distress—Psalm 29, 42, 44, 71, 88, 109, 113
  Need for healing—Psalm 22, 38, 41
  Need for guidance—Psalm 25, 37, 72
  Need for justice—Psalm 26, 52, 114
  Need for forgiveness—Psalm 39, 51

- Write a free-form psalm based on your feeling or longing. If you prefer, choose a psalm that expresses some of what you are feeling and rewrite it in your own words. Be as honest with God as the psalmists are.
- Read your psalm aloud to yourself. Pray it. Offer it to God.

Tip

Keep your Psalm in a journal or other safe place. Return to it if you need to express that same feeling in prayer again.

C h a p t e r   2

BASIC CONTEMPLATIVE PRACTICES

OUR CULTURE rewards those who move quickly and effi-ciently and think on their feet. We are surrounded by so many voices clamoring for our attention that it is difficult to zero in on any one voice. It is hard to listen deeply to one another, let alone to that "still, small voice" that we associate with God. In classic Christian spirituality, the way to do that is to slow down, calm down, be still and silent, turning our awareness and attention to signs of God's presence—the "fruit of the Spirit" described in Paul's letter to the Galatians (5:22-23), which includes love, joy, peace, gentleness, goodness, faith, meekness, and temperance.

Contemplation is the stillness we need to be aware of God's pres-ence. Jesuit theologian Walter Burghart calls it "the long, loving look at the Real."[1] It is long because our relationship with God (like our relationships with people) takes time; we must devote ample time to this Person we love. It is loving because we need to shed our judg-ments and fears and open ourselves to love just as we are. It is a look because we must face it. Denial is the enemy. And it is the Real because God is not interested in phoniness. We are being invited by God to look at our lives as they are, not as we would like them to be. Therefore, whatever is real to us is what we bring to contempla-tion and awareness before God. It need not be something high and mighty or a matter of only the gravest concern. It need only be what is real to us right now.

As you read this, you may be saying to yourself, "This chapter is not for me—I'm just not contemplative by nature." Before you hastily make that assumption, consider that contemplation is not a personality trait, such as introversion. Many highly introverted people are contemplative but so are many highly extroverted people. Anyone can take a "long, loving look at the Real," whether they are quiet and introspective or chatty and outward-directed. You do not have to be a pro at sitting in silence, although taking time to be in silence (even for a few minutes) is helpful in contemplation. Some activities listed here involve a lot of silence, and others are interspersed with silence. If you find silence troubling, start with small doses and see if your comfort level doesn't shift somewhat over time.

Maybe you're wondering, "Why be contemplative?" A short answer is that, as Christians, we follow the path of Jesus, and we notice that he takes many opportunities for time-out to be with God. Benedictine sister Joan Chittister says, "Contemplatives are people whose consciousness of God permeates their entire lives."[2] With that definition, I think we can safely name Jesus as a contemplative.

It is helpful to reject the old, false notion that prayer and contemplation are on one end of a spectrum with action on the other. Obviously, Jesus was a man of action. There is a natural spiritual flow between the journey inward (contemplation) and the journey outward (service and action). One enhances and enriches the other. In fact, most contemplatives agree that if their time in the presence of God does not in some way draw them to a life of reaching out to others in some way, then they are way offtrack.

What if fear and anxiety surface in prayer? At its heart, contemplation is a movement from fear to love. However, when people who are used to living "full tilt" slow down—observing silence and cultivating awareness—there is always the chance that fear and anxiety will emerge. This is perfectly normal, and yet when it happens, it can be upsetting. It is not a cause for all-out rejection of contemplative practices, for in fact any prayer practice, Bible study, or spiritual experience could trigger the same reaction. Taking a "long, loving look at the Real" involves facing our fears and moving past them to embrace God's love.

If any of these activities draw you to a fearful place, first set the activity aside and breathe deeply for a few moments. Visualize yourself basking in the love of God. Observe your physical and emotional reactions. You might want to write in a journal about the experience. Then you might want to seek a spiritual director or trusted friend to talk with about the experience. You can always go back to an activity at a later time.

"Here I Am" Prayer

If you are a beginner to contemplative prayer or if you want to get back to basics, there is no better place to start than with this simple prayer adapted from Anthony Bloom's classic *Beginning to Pray*. Bloom, a Russian Orthodox archbishop who died in 2003, wrote this short book in 1970, and it continues to be an inspiration today. In his chapter "Managing Time," Bloom describes this prayer exercise in narrative form.[3] I've broken it down into steps. It is so simple and short that it can be used daily as a prelude to other prayer practices.

Intention

To be here now in prayer.

The Exercise

- Resolve to be in prayer for at least five minutes. Do not answer the phone or allow yourself to be distracted from your goal.
- Be seated and say to yourself, "Here I am seated, doing nothing. I will do nothing for five minutes" (or longer, depending on the time you set for yourself).
- Begin noticing your own bodily presence—how your body feels next to the chair; how your feet feel against the floor. Relax your body. Notice what you feel inside.
- Now notice the presence of all that is around you. Say to yourself, "Here I am in the presence of the room (garden, chapel, wherever you are)." Be aware of the furniture, walls, and any pets or people in the room. Just be present and silent in your environment. Relax even more.

- Now say to yourself, "Here I am in the presence of God." Repeat silently to God, "Here I am." Bask in the presence of the Holy One until your time goal has been reached.

Tip

Feel free to move the steps around. You may want to start by noticing God's presence. The progression could also move from your environment to your body to God's presence. I find that I usually need to settle my body down first in order to be still enough to be present to God.

Centering Prayer

The term *centering prayer* is sometimes used to describe any prayer that centers us and grounds us in God as we move into other prayers or prayer practices. However, for a growing number of Christians, centering prayer is a term that describes one specific prayer practice that is *apophatic*, which means wordless, imageless, and wholly contemplative. For the purposes of this book, when we speak of centering prayer, we are speaking of this particular prayer practice.

No one "invented" centering prayer, but in our time Father Thomas Keating, a Cistercian priest and founder of the centering prayer movement, has certainly popularized it. Keating points to the many mystics and holy people throughout the ages who referred to a kind of prayer in which "deep calls to deep" without words or imagery. Teresa of Avila (sixteenth century) called it "the prayer of Quiet." Keating writes, "Silence is God's first language; everything else is a poor translation."[4]

As you read how centering prayer is entered, you may notice that it looks a lot like mantra meditation or what some might call secular meditation. What makes it different is that centering prayer has as its sole intention to be in the presence of the living Creator.

If you find this type of prayer challenging, you are not alone. But don't give up just because it may be hard—or may feel as though you "aren't really praying." God knows your intention and honors it. Also, as

Keating points out in *Invitation to Love,* many of the benefits of centering prayer are reaped in insights, revelations, well-being, and commitment to action that comes at times when you are *not* in prayer.[5] Be patient and non-judgmental with this prayer. Above all, be gentle with yourself. Many Christians who discover this style of prayer find a freedom in their spiritual life that they did not know before centering prayer.

Intention

To be still and know God's presence.

The Exercise

- Decide about how long you wish to stay in centering prayer. If you're a beginner and are not accustomed to silence, you might want to start with ten minutes. Most advocates of centering prayer recommend at least twenty minutes, with thirty minutes as a good amount to aim for on a regular basis. You may keep a clock close by to check the time or—if you think you might be tempted to focus too much on the time if you look at the clock—set an alarm. Either way, let go of concerns about the time.
- Choose a word that fits your image of God, Christ, or the Holy Spirit. Any word will do. You needn't worry about picking the best word—just something that is meaningful. This will be your sacred word for the next few minutes.
- Find a comfortable position in your chair. Feel free to shift your weight now and then to remain comfortable.
- Ask the living presence of Christ to become real to you in this time of centering prayer. Take a few moments of silence to focus on your intention.
- Say your sacred word to yourself silently. Allow your word to be the only thought in your mind. Other thoughts will come and go, but gently return to your word, silently repeating your word to yourself—not frantically, but in a relaxed way. If another thought comes into your head, simply acknowledge it and go back to your word.

- Even if you find yourself wanting to use other words to express yourself to God, go back to your word. You will have time later to say what you need to say to God in words.
- When the time you have set is over, end this centering prayer by thanking God for the gift of silence and presence. Silently say any words you longed to say to God before.
- You may choose to spend some time after the prayer reflecting and writing in a journal about the experience. What was it like for you? What was the hardest part of the prayer? What part of the prayer seemed effortless? What was going on inside your mind? What feelings did it bring up? Did you feel closer to God as a result? How does it feel to move from thoughts to silence? How does awareness change as we stop what we are doing? Would you do this prayer again, on your own or in a group? Do you think twenty minutes (or whatever amount you chose) is a long time to spend in silence? Why or why not?

Tips

Distractions and a wandering mind are to be expected during this prayer. Let not your heart be troubled! Simply return to your word. Over time, you will find deep spaces of silence opening between the repeating of your word.

Many Catholic parishes offer "drop-in" centering prayer groups weekly. Some people prefer practicing centering prayer with others.

Deep Listening

There's hardly a self-help, pop psychology, or leadership development book on the market that doesn't emphasize our need to listen far more than we speak. Similarly, the heart of Christian spiritual contemplation is listening—to the still, small voice of God, to our inner wisdom, and to others. This exercise will assist you in listening for "the heart of the matter" as other people are sharing with you.

Listening in this fashion takes practice. Most of us listen to other people just long enough to formulate our witty or "helpful" responses. That's not deep listening. That's conversational back-and-forth. It has its place, but it's not what this exercise is about. You may find as you practice this exercise that it is challenging, especially since there are simple guidelines that need to be followed specifically.

Try to approach the guidelines with openness, understanding that they were developed based on experience and are designed to help us rein in our learned tendency to prefer talking to listening. Once you master the tendency to formulate a response while someone else is talking, you may want to try this deep listening in everyday life. As your best friend or partner tells about his or her day, just listen with an open heart. As your child rambles on and on about playtime, simply listen and surround the listening with prayer.

Intention

To listen prayerfully and intently to another person's story.

The Exercise

- This exercise is designed to be done with another person. Find someone in your family or circle of friends who agrees to a listening session with you. Explain ahead of time how the process will go. Make sure your listening partner understands that this is a slow and sometimes silent process, and it's perfectly normal to have long pauses during the sharing time.

- Explain to your listening partner that you will be taking turns sharing a memory. There is a simple guideline for listening: when the time comes for one person to share, the other person will listen and pray silently for the other person's story, with no interrupting, interjecting, or gesturing. The listener remains silent and fixed on the speaker's story at all times.

- Settle into your chairs and get comfortable. Decide who will keep an eye on the time.

- Begin with a short prayer, asking God to assist you in listening, sharing, and deepening the memory. Ask for insight and compassion.

- Recall a time when you experienced God's presence. If that seems too difficult, then recall a time when you experienced deep and abiding love.
- Spend about ten minutes in silence with that memory, allowing it to reverberate in your mind and heart.
- Turn to your listening partner and ask that person to share their memory first. When one person is sharing, *the other is listening and silently praying for the memory to be deepened.* Avoid interrupting or making any verbal, or even physical response. Just watch and listen. Then, when the first person is finished sharing (about 10 minutes), say thank you and return to a few moments of silence.
- Now it is time for you to share your memory and have the other person become the listener. Again, the listener remains silent and attentive. About ten minutes is allowed for this memory to be shared. At the end, the listener says thank you.
- After both people have shared, reflect on the experience together. What was it like to be listened to? What was it like to listen and pray at the same time? How does deep listening enhance the experience for the one being listened to? What are some ways you might incorporate deep listening into your daily life?
- Say a short final prayer of thanksgiving for the time together.

Tip

It is difficult to simply listen. Don't beat yourself up if you slip up and interject something while your partner is sharing. But also, resolve to return to "deep listening mode," recommitting yourself to following the guideline.

Prayer of the Heart

Deep within each of us is a prayer phrase longing to be expressed, what some have named the Prayer of the Heart. It consists of two simple phrases—one said on inhalation and one said on exhalation. Early Christians used to pray, "Come, Lord Jesus," in this fashion. That was their deep longing, for Jesus to return and be among them in physical reality. We will spend time in this exercise finding those prayers that are as close to us as our very breath. The beauty of this prayer is the way it stays with you all day, all week, or even for a life-time if you allow it.

Intention

To discover and pray our own Prayer of the Heart.

The Exercise

- Begin seated in a comfortable position. Make sure your body weight is distributed in such a way that you feel stable. Take about five deep, slow breaths and allow the tension of the day to flow out with each exhalation. After five deliberate breaths, turn your attention away from counting and allow your breath to find its natural pace.

- What is your deepest and truest longing for life with God at this moment? If you find that your longing feels "tacky" or too worldly, try suspending judgment and instead looking at what's at the base of that desire. When you check in with your deepest and truest self, what it is that you seek from God?

- Give that longing a short phrase. For example, if your deep desire is inner freedom, then your phrase would be "freedom" or "inner freedom." Make sure your phrase is not too long.

- What is your favorite name for God? How do you image the Creator? Choose whatever name seems to fit best for you. Some examples include: Jesus, Wisdom, Father, Mother, or Mystery. Be as creative as you want to be. But again, keep the name rather short.

- Combine your name for God with your longing. For example, if my phrase is "freedom" and the name I choose for God is Christ, my prayer of the heart might be "Freedom, in Christ." Spend a few moments coming up with your two-part prayer.

- Begin to say—either aloud or silently—your phrase. You may inhale on the name for God and exhale on the desire or vice versa. Spend several minutes breathing this prayer. Make it your own. Allow God to inhabit this prayer.

- After several minutes of repeating this prayer, sink into contemplative silence. Allow the love of God to fill you and surround you.
- If you want to be sure to remember this phrase to pray it throughout the day, write it down. You might want to place it on the back of a business card and put it in your wallet or pocket. Place it on a sticky note next to your computer, or on the door of your refrigerator.

Tip

The moment we start to notice our breath, we invariably begin to control it. The goal in any breathing meditation is to inhale and exhale naturally, without trying to control our body's natural pace. The point of taking five deliberate breaths is to consciously slow down. Once you move on to the phrases, let your body set the pace for the breath.

The Jesus Prayer

This is one of the most famous prayers in the history of Christianity. You will find a version of it in the Gospel of Luke in the story of the Pharisee and the tax collector (18:13). Jesus praised the tax collector for humbling himself in prayer, saying, "God, be merciful to me, a sinner!" Christians later expanded the prayer to "Lord Jesus Christ, Son of God, have mercy on me, a sinner." In the Gospel of Mark, blind Bartimaeus cries out to Jesus, "Son of David, have mercy on me" (Mark 10:47). Orthodox Christians in the Middle Ages popularized this prayer, believing that the name of Jesus was a source of power and grace leading to a state of inner silence known as *hesychia*. In short, this prayer—though sometimes spoken—led them to a place of deep contemplation or centering prayer.[6]

Today many people find the Jesus Prayer to be the ultimate "prayer of the heart." Some repeat it silently as they take long walks. Others use it to lead them into contemplation. Some popular versions include "Jesus, have mercy on me"; "Lord Jesus Christ, have mercy on me"; and the simple "Christ, have mercy." As the Reverend Daniel Wolpert points out in *Creating a Life with God,* "The exact wording, so long as it contains the name of Jesus, is irrelevant."[7]

Intention

To experience the power in repeatedly praying the name of Jesus.

The Exercise

- Decide how long you want to spend in this prayer.
- Choose a variation of the Jesus Prayer that suits you best:

  "Lord Jesus Christ, Son of God, have mercy on me, a sinner."
  "Lord Jesus Christ, have mercy on me."
  "Jesus, have mercy."
  "Christ, have mercy."

- You may find a comfortable seated position, or you may choose to walk around while engaged in this prayer.
- Breathe naturally and repeat the Jesus Prayer silently for the length of time you have chosen.
- When distractions crop up, return to the prayer.
- When your time is up, reflect on your experience of the Jesus Prayer. Describe your experience. (You may want to write in a journal on this.) How did you notice the presence of God or Christ in this prayer? What is the value of repeating this prayer over and over silently? Did you notice any inner movements within your spirit as you prayed this prayer?
- End with a short prayer of gratitude.

Tips

It is natural for people who first pray the Jesus Prayer to feel that they "aren't doing it right." Silent, repetitive prayers like the Jesus Prayer and centering prayer are not goal oriented. Distractions are perfectly normal. If you return to your phrase consistently, you are doing it right. There's not much more to it than that.

Think of this less as a discipline you have to conquer and more as a way of opening yourself to God's wide mercy and love. The repetition soothes our soul and relaxes our bodies to be more receptive to God.

Praying with Icons

When our intention is to seek God's presence, one effective mode of prayer is gazing at an object as a window to the unseen God—be it a traditional religious icon or an object we've chosen because of its meaning for us. Perhaps you've had the experience of gazing at something in nature that fascinates you. Simply looking, without assigning any particular interpretation or meaning to the object of your gaze, can take you deep into contemplative awareness of God.

Icons—usually flat paintings on wood but also mosaics, frescos, embroideries, or statues—have a long and contentious history in Byzantine Christianity. In the eighth and ninth centuries, a vicious controversy grew between Christians who took literally the Jewish mandate that there be no image of God venerated and Christians who used images of Jesus, Mary, and the saints in prayer. In 730 c.e., Emperor Leo II banned the use of icons and commanded they be destroyed. Many Christians refused to go along with this edict, arguing that since God the Son took on flesh and became incarnate, the use of physical matter to depict God's son or holy people would be acceptable. Today, almost every Orthodox Christian household has an icon corner or shelf where the family stops to pray.[8]

If you're interested in praying with icons, you may be wondering where to find one. Many beautiful replicas of ancient icons are available in religious bookstores or online. New icons are being written (that's the term for the painting or creation of an icon) every day, and if you purchase original icons you can be sure the writers have spent hours in prayer as they put paint on the wood or paper of the image you are looking at. Lots of books carry pictures of icons. And you can certainly find many beautiful images of icons on the Internet with a simple search.

I suggest beginning this exercise by using a traditional icon (or copy of one). That's because they are lovingly created expressly for the purpose of prayer, and praying with one binds you to the great cloud of witnesses that have prayed with these images throughout history. But there is no restriction on what images you may use. A photograph or painting that you treasure would also suffice. The important part is seeking God's presence. The image in front of you is merely a window to God.

Intention

To seek God's presence with the assistance of a sacred image.

The Exercise

- Find a comfortable place to sit and gaze at your chosen icon. Decide how long you will spend in this contemplative practice. (20 minutes is suggested.)
- Express your intention to encounter God. Ask God for guidance.
- In Orthodox spirituality, we are invited to allow our mind to descend deep into the center of our heart, where we will encounter the presence of God. Spend a few moments pondering this, and try allowing it to happen.
- Gaze at the icon. Let your gaze be long and loving. Think of the icon as a mystical window in which you are on one side and God is on the other. Allow God to communicate with you by way of this image, but do not become anxious about *how* or *when* God may communicate. Simply continue to gaze and allow your heart to become still and open. Do this until you reach your time limit.

- End the contemplation with a prayer of gratitude.
- Spend a few minutes reflecting on the experience. Did you understand or feel that your mind descended into your heart? What was it like to use your eyes so intently in prayer? Did you feel the presence of the Holy during this prayer? If so, can you describe what you felt or experienced? Were there any expectations on your part for this prayer? Would you be inclined to pray in this way again? Why or why not?

Tips

A beautiful small book on praying with icons by Henri Nouwen includes four lovely prints of Russian icons. *Behold the Beauty of the Lord* (Ave Maria Press, 1987) is a treasure for those who want to learn more about praying with icons.

For a brief and easily digestible recap of the icon controversy, I recommend Bradley Holt's *Thirsty for God,* second edition (Fortress Press, 2005). It's in the chapter on "The European Era."

Contemplative Work Process

As you become familiar with contemplative practices, you will want to bring this new awareness into the way you conduct your life's business. The contemplative work process is designed to put first things first, combining deep listening with prayer and reflection. It involves a flow from inward reflection to outward reflection, culminating in action. Work is the last step.

Mark Yaconelli, codirector of the Youth Ministry and Spirituality Project, promoted this process for all deliberations the project conducted. He called the process "Liturgy for Business Meetings." He found that work was completed far more efficiently after the group had spent time in contemplative prayer than in traditional business meetings, where people were more focused on their agendas than on the presence of God.

For individuals, this process is used alone as you work on a particular task. It can also be used with a partner, with a friend, or with a group—anywhere the work of listening and problem solving needs to take place.

Intention

To transform a work task by surrounding it with prayer.

The Exercise

- Begin your time with a ritual that recognizes God. Light a candle, sing a chant, or begin with a short prayer.
- Proceed to a time of "checking in." If you are alone, spend a few minutes thinking about how you are feeling at this time. Are you preoccupied with thoughts about another matter? If you are in a group, spend time allowing each person to share what's going on in his or her life. Practice deep listening with no interrupting or commenting, and allow silence between speakers. After everyone has had the opportunity to check in, move on to the next step.
- Engage in one of the prayer exercises in this book. *Lectio divina*, the examen, and centering prayer are recommended. (About 20 minutes)
- What did you notice about the presence of God during the prayer practice? If in a group, practice the "deep listening" guideline—one person speaks at a time with no interrupting or commenting on what is said.
- Attend to the *purpose* of the work. Without yet beginning the actual work, reflect on the task at hand. What is the invitation or call from God here?
- Attend to the work task. Out of the listening and prayer, begin the work. Continue to be aware of the listening, the prayer, and the call from God as you do the work.
- End the time of work with a closing prayer, offering yourself and your efforts to God.

Tip

You might want to compare the quality of your work done in this manner to a day or meeting in which you did not attend so carefully and intentionally to yourself and to God.

Even if tempted, do not skip the check-in or the prayer steps. They are crucial to clearing out the inner space for God's work to be done.

Chapter 3

LECTIO DIVINAS

THE PRACTICE of *lectio divina,* which is Latin for "sacred reading," continues to gain in popularity as people discover anew this ancient and meaningful approach to prayer. We can thank the Benedictine Order in the Catholic Church for this legacy. Benedict of Nursia (fifth century) asked his order to spend considerable time in prayer with Scripture, poring over it, repeating it, and listening as each word and phrase settled into the heart. Benedict, however, did not "invent" this practice, as M. Basil Pennington reminds us in his book *Lectio Divina*: "In fact, it is a very ancient reality. It is part of the rich heritage we received from our Jewish sisters and brothers."[1]

There are many variations of *lectio divina,* which is why we include several exercises for this one type of prayer. All of them are contemplative, inviting that "long, loving look" at some discrete aspect of life—be it Scripture, a poem, music, or nature. As we look at this "text," we listen, as the Benedictines instructed, "with the ear of the heart," for a word, phrase, sound, or image that holds, for us, a word from God. This could be a word of comfort, instruction, challenge, or assurance. It could be an image suggested by a word, and the image could take us to a place of deep reverence or personal introspection. Pennington likens *lectio divina* to a person choosing a tasty morsel of food from a banquet table and savoring that one bite for all its flavor and nutrition.[2] Throughout our day, we might return to the taste of that morsel, remembering the goodness and meaning found in such a small bite.

It is important to note that, like the biblical exercises in this book, *lectio divina* is about what is evoked in you as you experience the text. Now is not the time for historical-critical musings or scholarly interpretations of the text. It's time for falling in love with the Word and experiencing the goodness of God. Some preachers and biblical scholars find *lectio divina* a helpful prayer practice to engage in prior to digging in and drawing meaning from the text. With that in mind, you might try *lectio divina* on a Scripture passage before it is read in worship (easy to do if your liturgy includes readings from the common lectionary or if the texts are announced in advance) or before you approach it in Bible study. It may give you a greater depth of experience with the Word.

Take your time with each of these exercises. Enjoy a leisurely pace. Don't force anything—allow the word, phrase, sound, or image to come to you in due time.

Lectio Divina

This is a traditional five-step method for *lectio divina* with Scripture, complete with its Latin terms. Some versions you may run across include only four steps (not counting the introductory silence as the first step) and other versions will show the steps in a different order (sometimes transposing the fourth and fifth step). The steps can be changed somewhat; however, I find this particular order has a nice rhythm to it as it opens and closes with silence.

Some people find, after doing this form of *lectio divina* over a long period of time, that they naturally fall into each step as they slowly ponder Scripture. Try this every day for a month and see if you don't internalize the steps and fall in love with this form of communication with God.

Intention

To experience a word from God in God's Word.

The Exercise

- Step One: *Silencio*. After choosing your Scripture and placing it nearby, become still and quiet within. Silently turn all your thoughts and desires over to God. Let go of concerns, worries, or agendas. Just *be* for a few minutes.

- Step Two: *Lectio.* Read your short passage slowly and carefully, either aloud or silently. Reread it. Be alert to any word, phrase, or image that seems to have energy for you. It could be a word that invites you, a phrase that puzzles you, an image that intrigues you. Wait for this word, phrase, or image to speak to you; do not rush or force it. Read the passage as many times as you like.

- Step Three: *Meditatio.* Take whatever word, phrase, or image from your Scripture passage that has energy for you and allow yourself to ponder it in your heart. In this phase, we ruminate over our chosen text. Repeat it to yourself like a mantra. Allow this word, phrase, or image to interact with your deepest self—your thoughts, desires, memories. Let it speak to your life.

- Step Four: *Oratio.* Let your soul be deeply in prayer, allowing God to transform you through the word, phrase, or image from Scripture. Let your feelings be open and honest with God. Let your heart be in dialogue with God. Consider how this word, phrase, or image connects with your life today. How is God present to you in it?

- Step Five: *Contemplatio.* Rest silently in the presence of God. Move beyond words, phrases, or images. Enjoy the freedom that comes in contemplation.

- If you desire, write about this prayer experience in a journal. What is your word, phrase, or image? What does God reveal to you in it? What does it have to say about your life right now?

Tips

You may want to use one of the other simple contemplation exercises from this book for Step One (*silencio*). Try the "Here I Am" exercise or the centering prayer.

Don't be frustrated if, for some reason, you don't find a word, phrase, or image that seems to be revealing something of God to you. It happens to almost everyone who does *lectio divina* at one time or another. Sometimes it's from trying too hard, so let go of having to "perform" in this exercise. Sometimes it is the Scripture that is chosen. When it happens, move through the steps without a word, phrase, or image and allow yourself simply to be in the presence of God. You'll be effectively jumping ahead to Step Five (*contemplatio*), which is fine.

Also be aware that sometimes the word that has energy for you is a word that disturbs you. Simply take the disturbance into prayer and allow God to reveal to you what the tension is about. It is more important to be honest in prayer than it is to attempt to find a comfortable word.

Lectio Divina on Community

Now that you've experienced *lectio divina* with Scripture, you are ready to try it in different situations, using life itself as a "text." This is a creative approach to *lectio divina*, although it is a natural step that most people who practice *lectio divina* take as they learn the practice. As you pray with Scripture in this fashion, you will notice that you begin looking for "words, phrases, or images" throughout your day that shimmer with possibility for revelation from God.

Since we are all connected in many ways to a variety of communities, it is helpful to reflect, in prayer, on experiences we have in community. You could select a meeting you recently attended, a worship service, or a family reunion. The community you choose could be your family, your workplace, your faith community, even a circle of friends. This event in the life of your community will be the "text" you ponder as you search for a word from God.

Intention

Seeking God's presence and direction in our connections with community.

The Exercise

- Step One: *Silencio*. Enter your time of prayer in silence, committing all that you are and all you desire right now to God. As you breathe and slow down, become aware of God's presence.
- Step Two: *Lectio*. Spend time reviewing an event in the life of a community or group you are part of. Let what happened in that event roll in your imagination much like a videotape plays a scene. As you remember this time in community, what "shimmers" for you? What relationships and experiences come to you? What part of the event stands out? What invites more reflection? What seems to have energy for you? It could be a word, phrase, statement, action, image, or sound. Just notice what part of that memory is inviting you to spend more time with it.
- Step Three: *Meditatio*. Let your mind, body, and spirit be present to the experience you chose to reflect on. What does this experience have to offer you? How does it make your body feel? What moods does it evoke in you?
- Step Four: *Oratio*. Based on what you ruminated on in the *meditatio* step, what do you want to say to God about this remembered experience? Offer all your thoughts, feelings, and reflections to God. Allow God to interact with you in the experience.
- Step Five: *Contemplatio*. Allow all that you are to sink into God's loving embrace. Move beyond all thoughts and feelings and be still and silent.
- If you desire, write about this prayer experience in a journal. What does the memory reveal to you? How is God present to you? How is God present in the community you are connected to?

Tips

It is helpful to decide before the prayer begins what experience you are going to reflect on—that way you aren't spending a lot of time seeking out a "life text" to pray over.

You may find yourself wanting to return to this prayer exercise at times when a life event rattles you or fills you with awe. It's a great way to get out of the rut of worry or anxiety about an event and into the creative act of prayer.

Luther's Four-stranded Garland

Reformation leader Martin Luther (1483–1546), who was once an Augustinian monk, described what we would call a form of *lectio divina* in his book *A Simple Way to Pray.*[3] To practice this form, think of a garland or ribbon with four strands, each of which represents a way of listening to the Scripture: instruction, thanksgiving, confession, and guidance. Luther suggested that, when reading Scripture, we pray with the Scripture by allowing a word, phrase, or image to speak to us in those four different ways.[4]

As with other forms of *lectio divina*, you will first notice what, in the Scripture, seems to have energy for you. Then you will put a series of questions to that word, phrase, or image.

Of all the forms of *lectio divina*, this one is a bit more analytical or heady. Still, make sure you spend adequate time with silence and enjoy the *contemplatio* phase at the end.

Intention

To allow Scripture to speak words of instruction, thanksgiving, confession, and guidance.

The Exercise

- Choose the passage of Scripture you want to pray with. As before, make sure it is relatively short.

- Ask God to be present in this prayer. Begin with a few moments of silence.
- Read through the Scripture at least two times, aloud if that helps. Be alert for something in it—a word, phrase, or image— that feels weighted with importance for you. It could be something that stands out in your mind, "shimmers," or intrigues you in some way.
- Repeat your word, phrase, or image to yourself (*meditatio*) for a few minutes. Allow it to settle into your heart.
- What, in that word, phrase, or image, seems to have a lesson for you? You may want to write down the lesson or instruction.
- What, in your chosen word, phrase, or image, brings out a sense of gratitude and thanksgiving in you? Write this down if you want.
- What draws you to confess a sin, shortcoming, or other spiritual block that stands between you and a healthy relationship with God? Again, you may want to write in a journal about this.
- Read the passage again. See if something in it feels like a word of guidance in your life. Notice how God is present in Scripture, and how God might be leading you.
- Silently sink into that place beyond words, phrases, or images and rest in the presence of God (*contemplatio*). Stay there as long as you desire.
- Close with a spoken or silent prayer, thanking God for being alive and present in your understanding of this Scripture.

Tip

If you are a crafts lover, you might want to create your own four-stranded garland to remind you of the steps. You could glue or sew together four colorful ribbons and use them as a bookmark in your Bible. Or you could buy a wide ribbon and cut four strands, leaving the ribbon whole at the top.

Lectio Divina with Music

Music lovers are in for a treat with this prayer. Instead of listening for a word from the written page, you will be listening for what is evoked in you by the music. You are allowing God to speak to you through musical notes, phrases, and images.

The choice of music used in this prayer is entirely up to you. It can be instrumental or vocal. It can be from any genre that inspires you—it does not have to be religious or from the inspirational genre. If you have a music collection, start with a selection that has moved you in some way previously.

After doing this prayer intentionally for awhile, you may find yourself moved to prayer spontaneously when listening to music. That's the beauty of *lectio divina*—it becomes a part of life as you practice it regularly. It helps us "pray always."

Intention

To experience God in music.

The Exercise

- Choose the music you want to pray with.
- Begin with silence, asking God to be present in the music.
- Listen to your selection more than once. As you do this, be aware of any image, word, emotion, or memory that is called forth in you.
- When you settle on an image, word, emotion, or memory, sit silently with it and bring your attention back to it when your attention strays. Allow this prayer gift to deepen in you.
- What might this image, word, phrase, or emotion have to say about your life today? How is it connected to your spiritual journey? Ask God to reveal that to you.
- Rest silently with your image, word, phrase, or emotion. Offer it to God. Wait patiently on God.
- What would you like to express to God about the experience of praying with this piece of music? You might want to write in a journal about it, share it with someone, or return to it in prayer at another time.

- Settle into a wordless and imageless time with God. When distractions get in the way, simply acknowledge them and return to *contemplatio*.
- Thank God for what is received in this time of prayer.

Tip

This prayer will be easier for some people than for others. In traditional *lectio divina,* we have a lot of words to work with. With music—especially instrumentals—we don't have word hooks to grab on to. We are propelled into the ephemeral world of emotion, images, and memories. Perhaps what comes to you is a word. But more likely it will be a feeling that leads you to a memory or an image. Whatever feels important to you is what you take into prayer and spend time on with God.

Lectio Divina in Nature

The grandeur of nature frequently draws us to God. St. Francis of Assisi (thirteenth century) spoke of a deep love of nature in his "Canticle of the Sun" in which he wrote, "Be thou praised, my Lord, for brother Wind and for the air, the cloud, the serene and all kinds of weather, by which thou givest thy creatures sustenance."[5] Few of us live as close to nature as the beggar-preacher Francis did. In fact, our busy contemporary lives keep us closed up in climate-controlled boxes much of the time, avoiding messy weather and pesky bugs.

This exercise, however, helps us deepen our connection with God in creation. This *lectio divina* with nature is adapted from an exercise spiritual director Nancy Wiens shared with the Youth Ministry and Spirituality Project in 2001. Nancy frequently leads groups on retreats that place them in silence with creation—unfettered by walls or even tent coverings—to experience *lectio divina* over days at a time.

Wiens emphasizes that too often we think of ourselves as apart from nature. "We, too, are nature—the human part of nature that has the ability to be self-conscious and make choices by enacting free will. So, praying in the outdoors of nature helps us connect with our human nature before God."

I've found that this prayer can open people to experiences of God in ways that spoken prayers or word prayers did not do before.

Intention

To experience the magnificence of nature, God in nature, and ourselves as nature.

The Exercise

- Step One: *Silencio.* Become present to your surroundings in nature by sitting in silence for a few moments. Ask God to address you in this prayer through nature.
- Step Two: *Lectio.* Look around you. Take some time to walk around and survey the piece of creation that surrounds you. As you do this, notice when something draws your attention. It could be something attractive or something that repulses or upsets you. Just look for something that has some energy for you. As you gaze on it, imagine God also gazing on it.
- Step Three: *Meditatio.* Continue to be with this part of nature that has drawn your attention. Think about what you know about this part of nature. What are the connections you might make with your life right now? Be aware of your feelings as well as your thoughts. What is God saying to you in this encounter with nature?
- Step Four: *Oratio.* Express yourself in some way to God. Respond to God's gift in nature in some way. Express your experience to God—your feelings, bodily sensations, and thoughts. Resist editing them. Simply communicate with God.
- Step Five: *Contemplatio.* Rest with God in what you notice, and reflect on how that awareness speaks to your life. Open your whole self to God by moving beyond words and images. Bask in what God has done in you during this prayer. Bask in how your human nature has communed with the rest of nature and also with God.

Tips

You may want to write in a journal throughout this prayer or after it.

If, for any reason, you cannot be outdoors and want to pray in this way, simply gaze out a window or even sit indoors with a plant or pet. Nature is in and around us. Inclement weather or circumstances that keep us housebound will not stop God from addressing us in nature.

Use this prayer when you are traveling or on vacation. Take time to pray in this way and you'll experience your surroundings—and God—in a new and more profound way.

Chapter 4

LIFE REFLECTIONS

THE STORY of our life unfolds as we make crucial choices, cope with unexpected challenges, and seek stability in the midst of change. Within this story are glimpses of God's loving guidance, companionship, and support along the way—if, as Jesus says, we have eyes to see.

We develop these special eyes by looking at chapters in the story or episodes in our lives. Isolating manageable pieces (a day, week, month, season, or event) and applying memory and wisdom in the context of prayer many times unveils a blessing, or at the very least a sense of context for our lives.

Some of the prayers in this chapter may be quite familiar to you. Others may be new. Each one invites you to explore an aspect of your life for traces of the Divine. This kind of exploration is worthwhile in and of itself. Beyond that, however, it is the foundation of all spiritual discernment—that is, exploring God's purpose for your life in determining the steps you will take and the choices you will make in the future. So the more familiar you are with reflecting on your life in prayer, the more equipped you will be to do the work of discernment.

Many of the prayers in this chapter are attributed to Ignatius of Loyola, founder of the Roman Catholic Jesuit order (sixteenth century). He may or may not have originated any of these exercises, but we are certain of the extraordinary gift he gave in writing them down, ensuring that generations of people who came after him would know about and benefit from these prayers. If you happen upon a translation of

Ignatius's work, you will find I have adapted these exercises with a much different language—as do many present-day enthusiasts of Ignatian spirituality. Pastoral counselor and spiritual director Donald St. Louis says that in years past, some of these exercises became for many people "a moralistic exercise in self-scrutiny," in which they would list the sins they committed that day as well as moments they felt close to God.[1] We may use a different language and approach from Ignatius, but the intent will be similar—for us to see our lives, just as they are, as an arena of God's grace breaking into the world.

The Traditional Ignatian Examen

The motto in Ignatian spirituality is to "find God in all things." We do that by examining our life. The practice is called an *examen,* which simply means "examination."

At the beginning of Ignatius of Loyola's *Spiritual Exercises*—a series of activities used primarily in retreats to draw one closer to Christ—is a prayer designed to infuse the day with awareness of where you felt close to God and where you felt distant from God. He recommends it three times a day: upon rising, after the noon meal, and after supper. Many people today prefer to use this examen at the end of their day as a nighttime prayer.

This traditional form focuses primarily on where we fall short in our day. This is not meant to be a time of self-flagellation, but a time of letting go of all that stands between us and God.

Intention

To reflect on feelings of God's presence and feelings of God's absence over time.

The Exercise

- Begin by giving thanks to God for all the gifts you have received in life.
- Ask for grace to see yourself as you are in the light of God's love. Ask that all within you that is not in line with God's purpose for your life be released.

- Ask God to show you where God has been active in your life today. Review your day in the light of God's love. Where did you feel closest to God? Express your gratitude for those moments.
- Ask God to forgive you for those times you failed to reflect God's love and mercy today. Express your desire to turn back to God.
- Resolve, by God's grace, to commit to living out God's purpose in your life. If you need to make amends for something you have done, resolve to do so now.
- Close by saying the Lord's Prayer.

Tip

If you are interested in reading Ignatius in his own words, you can find his entire *Spiritual Exercises*, letters, and autobiography in *Ignatius of Loyola,* one of the Classics of Western Spirituality published by Paulist Press. If you want to read *about* Ignatian spirituality, there are a variety of books available now that reflect on a modern understanding of "finding God in all things." A good one to start with is *Eyes to See, Ears to Hear: An Introduction to Ignatian Spirituality* by David Lonsdale (Maryknoll, N.Y.: Orbis Books, 2000).

A Contemporary Examen

One of the most popular contemporary versions of the Ignatian examen is found in *Sleeping with Bread: Holding What Gives You Life,* a small book by Dennis Linn, Sheila Fabricant Linn, and Matthew Linn (Paulist, 1995). The Linns, retreat and conference leaders, prefer to ask two simple questions—that can be worded in many different ways—at the end of a day, week, month, or life event.[2] I've adapted this process to include a number of versions of the two questions, and you may even want to discover for yourself new questions that help you best reflect on where you were the most aware of God's presence in your day.

The beauty of this simple examen is its flexibility. Parents can do it with small children. Groups can use it to pray about their time together. Use the two questions informally in conversation with a friend as he or she is trying to figure out the next step in a life journey. Once you learn the examen, it easily can become a way of life.

Intention

To pray through events of our daily life.

The Exercise

- Make yourself comfortable and set aside some quiet time for this prayer. You may want to light a candle to signify the light of Christ illuminating your day.
- Rest in silence for a few moments.
- Ask God's Spirit to lead you through your day.
- Review your day.
  If you could relive any one moment that brought you joy, which would it be? What happened in that moment that made it so life-giving? Sit with that moment and allow it to give you life again. Offer your gratitude to God for that moment.
  If you could go back and change any one moment in your day, which would it be? What made that moment so difficult? Sit with that moment in the light of God's love and allow yourself to feel whatever emotion you have. Offer that moment to God for healing.
- Make a note of these two moments in your day.
- End by giving thanks to God for all the ways God has been with you—through the joy and the pain.

Tips

Under the "review your day" step, if for some reason the two questions listed above aren't helpful for you, try one of the following alternative pairs:

- For what today are you most grateful?
- For what today are you least grateful?

- When did you feel closest to God today?
- When did you feel the most distant from God today?

- When did you feel yourself opening to God's Spirit (love or peace)?
- When did you feel yourself blocked from God's Spirit (love or peace)?

- What was your day's high point?
- What was your day's low point?

- When did you feel yourself moving toward God?
- When did you feel yourself moving away from God?

A wonderful "retreat in daily life" is to commit to doing this simple examen nightly for a month or two, and write down your answers to the two questions—even if all you write is a word or two. At periodic intervals, review what you have written. As you do this, you will begin to see patterns in the way you experience God. This information will help you become more aware of God's presence and help you discern important life choices in the future.

Prayer of Remembrance

Paying attention to a memory can become for us a deep and meaningful prayer. As we relive an experience, we discover new aspects of it, of ourselves, and of God. Any one memory could have many gifts for us in our lifetime.

So, relax and open yourself to reexperiencing a time in your life. It could be an especially joyful time or it could be a difficult, challenging time, but this time invite the Presence of the Holy to sit with you.

Intention

To experience God's love through an event in life.

The Exercise

- Find a quiet, comfortable place to spend about forty-five minutes in silence. You may want to have a journal close by. Open with a simple prayer, asking God to be present in this time.
- Turn your attention to something in your life—a past event, an experience, a memory—that has been on your mind. It could be something that has been nagging at you. Or something that was so wonderful you want to spend time reliving it. Give yourself at least ten minutes to select your memory for reflection.
- Focus intently on this memory. In your mind's eye, relive the experience. Allow all your senses—touch, taste, smell, sight, and hearing—to experience the memory. Be aware of how God was present with you in the experience and also now in the remembering. Allow this memory to deepen and expand so that it becomes for you a window to God. Spend at least ten minutes in this remembering phase.
- Now shift your attention to the remembering prayer. Where was your soul or spirit most animated? Where did you experience either the most attraction to God or inner disturbance? Explore with God the feeling that seemed most active. Stay with that feeling for at least ten minutes.
- At this time, move into a conversation with God about what you experienced in the last two movements of this exercise. You may want to write your conversation down or stay in your imagination. You may also want to imagine one or more figures of the Trinity sitting with you in a circle holding a "colloquy"

or roundtable discussion. Feel free to invite other divine or biblical figures in on the conversation as well. This is *your* colloquy and you may invite whomever you desire for conversation. Pose a question to the figures or simply sit and listen to what they have to offer. You may also sit in silence with them. Spend at least fifteen minutes in this colloquy.

- End by thanking the colloquy partners and by saying a prayer of thanksgiving to God for the experience, the memory, and the gifts that came from the imaginative reflection.

Tips

Some people are more imaginative than others. If imagining yourself at a table or circle with divine figures makes you uncomfortable, simply hold a prayerful dialogue with God or Jesus. You don't have to get fancy with this exercise.

On the other hand, some people discover they are drawn closer to God when they allow their imagination to run free. If you are like that, you might want to invite a favorite biblical character, angelic figure, or saint into the last step of the exercise.

Remember that your mind's visual image of God, Jesus, or other figures only serves as a window to the mystery of God. You may experience God's touch and presence, but you are not in any way conjuring up any divine figure. God is already present and active in your prayer long before you visualize God.

Praying Ultimate Questions

Spirituality is merely a feel-good enterprise if it does not address the ultimate questions of our life. Theologian Clyde Crews contends that ultimate questions are ones that "concern the very foundation of my life and meaning."[3] These are the God questions that turn our attention from our individualist lives to our lives in community with God and with one another.

I've compiled a variety of questions from different sources. You may use these for writing in a journal, reflection, or discussion starters. What makes asking these questions a prayer is turning our intention toward listening to the truth that emerges as we ponder the questions. Be as honest in your responses to these questions as you can be—even if your honesty calls into question some previous beliefs or what you think the "approved" answer might be. If Jesus can ask God why God forsook him on the cross, we can have confidence that God can handle our honesty as well.

Intention

Spending time in prayer with questions that open us to God.

The Exercise

- Find a comfortable setting to spend time with a question.
- Look over the list of questions below and select the one you will be praying with.
- If you like to write your reflections, have a journal or writing material handy.
- Begin by asking God to be present to you in the midst of the question and your reflections on it.
- Spend at least twenty minutes in silence with your question.
- First, open yourself to the question.
- Allow your mind to settle and simply sit with the question for a few minutes.
- What comes to mind? What is attractive to you about the question? What is disturbing?
- How would you—at this time in your life—answer this question?
- How is God present to you in either the question or your reflection on the question?
- Close with a short prayer of gratitude for the gifts that come in "ultimate questions."

Some Questions to Ponder in the Exercise

Theological Questions

- What is it that you care most about in life?
- What is revelation from God? When have you experienced it?
- What is the meaning of the Trinity?
- What is the role of evil in a world created by God?
- How can we find God? How does God find us?
- What is the true nature of God?
- In what ways does God intervene in the world?
- What is it that reconciles us with God?
- What is eternal life?

Questions Jesus Asked

- Why are you afraid? (Matthew 8:26)
- What is it you want me to do for you? (Mark 10:36)
- My God, why have you forsaken me? (Mark 15:34)
- Why were you searching for me? (Luke 2:49)
- Why do you call me "Lord, Lord," and do not do what I tell you? (Luke 6:46)
- Where is your faith? (Luke 8:25)
- Who do you say that I am? (Luke 9:20)
- What is written in the law? (Luke 10:26)
- What is the kingdom of God like? (Luke 13:18)
- When the Son of Man comes, will he find faith on earth? (Luke 18:8)
- Why do you call me good? (Luke 18:19)
- What are you looking for? (John 1:38)
- Do you want to be made well? (John 5:6)
- Will you lay down your life for me? (John 13:38)
- Have you believed because you have seen me? (John 20:29)
- Do you love me? (John 21:17)

Questions on Spirituality [4]

- When have you felt God's presence most acutely in your life?
- How do you know when God is communicating with you?
- What is your deepest desire in life? How is God present in that desire?
- In what life activities do you experience God's presence on a regular basis?
- In what activities do you feel blocked from God's presence?
- When did you first notice God's presence in your life?
- Who was God for you when you were a child?
- What do you want most from God?
- Can you recall a time you felt resentful, angry, or afraid of God?
- Can you think of a time in which God intervened in your life?
- Are there patterns of events in your life? What does the pattern indicate to you?
- If you truly felt God's love and presence in your life today, how might your actions change?
- Can you think of a hard time in your life in which you were able to feel God's presence and guidance even in the midst of the pain?
- What event in your life changed the direction of your life?
- What are your particular spiritual gifts to the world?
- What brings you to prayer? Can you speak honestly and soulfully to God? How do you do that?

Questions on Community Life [5]

- Are the communities you're involved with aware of the presence of God in their midst? If so, how? If not, what stands in the way?
- What is your belief about human beings and our ability to do good and evil?
- What is the relationship you desire with the environment?
- When did you feel you contributed to the common good?
- When did you do justice? What was the outcome?
- When did you do mercy? What was the outcome?

- How do you feel about the communities you are a part of? Are they life-giving to you?
- What are the shared beliefs in the community you are most involved in?
- How is God working in and through the communities of your life?

Tips

Don't tackle too many of these at one sitting. In fact, one at a time is best. If prayer is to be about increasing awareness, then the more you can focus on the question the more you will be in prayer with it.

When doing this with others, it is important that everyone's theology and life experience be respected. Even if one person feels strongly that another's view is "unorthodox," it is not appropriate, *in the context of this exercise,* for views to be debated.

The Prayer Journal

For Protestants, there is a long tradition of journal-keeping as prayer. You may have noticed that in many of the previous exercises, you are encouraged, if you so desire, to write your reflections in a journal. That is one way to keep a prayer journal—to pray and then reflect on the fruit of your prayer.

Another way is to do like the English and American Puritans and record significant events in our lives and then reflect on the spiritual lessons in these events.[6] We can also write our prayers out in the journal and then return to those prayers over time to see how God has answered us.

Intention

To keep a record of our communication with God.

The Exercise

- Decide how you want to keep this journal. You may purchase a blank book or use loose-leaf paper held in a ringed notebook.
- Decide how often you will make notations in your journal. You may want to record insights from other prayer practices or write your prayers in the journal or both. Some people even keep notes from their dreams in their journal. It's a book that belongs to you and God. Do with it what feels best.
- Begin by asking God to be present and alive in this journal-keeping exercise.
- To explore spiritual growth based on events in your life, write about a significant event or happening in your daily life.

     How do you feel about that event?

     Where was God at work in the event?

     Where is God leading me now as a result of this event?

     How do my feelings change as I view the event in the light of God's love?

- To notice how God is active in your life, review your journal at regular intervals.

     What patterns or common themes do you notice?

     How does God get your attention?

     How has God answered your prayers?

     Assess how your relationship with God is emerging.

- Make notations about any common themes or patterns.
- Close each journal session with a prayer of gratitude.

Tip

Even if you feel you are not a writer, give this exercise a try. This is a prayer exercise, not a writing exercise. No one but you has to see what you've written. Even if you share journal findings with a group, it matters little how you wrote what you discovered. Share it in your own words instead of reading from the page.

Art as Prayer

Just as writing our prayers in the form of a journal can be meaningful, drawing, painting, sculpting, or using other forms of visual arts in prayer can be illuminating. Creating visual images can move us out of our usual patterns of ruminating and allow fresh new insights to emerge.

Please don't skip this exercise because you think you can't draw, paint, or otherwise create in an artistic fashion. This is not about what sort of artist you are, so give your inner critic some time off. This is about opening yourself to God's loving touch through visual expression.

The concepts for this prayer are adapted from Barbara Ganim and Susan Fox's book *Visual Journaling.*[7]

Intention

To explore feelings in prayer through visual renderings.

The Exercise

- Place your art supplies on the table in front of you.
- Settle yourself by breathing slowly in and out for at least five breaths. Allow each exhalation to complete itself naturally before inhaling. With each breath, imagine God's love and creativity flowing in and out of you.
- Think about a question that you have taken into prayer recently. Perhaps it's a situation in your life, or a question much like the ones in the exercise "Praying Ultimate Questions." Settle on a question, and write down a clear intention for your prayer based on this question. For example, if you have been troubled about an interaction with one of your friends, you might write, "I intend to explore my feelings about _____." You may write on your drawing or painting paper or somewhere else. Make sure your intention for the prayer is constantly before you.
- Once again, become still and quiet. Allow your imagination to offer an image that addresses your intention. Be patient and

wait on an image but don't force an image. If you have trouble at this stage, simply acknowledge your feelings to God and invite an image to appear.

- Draw, paint, sculpt, or otherwise craft a representation of the image that calls to you. It does *not* have to be an actual representation. It could be an image of what the situation feels like. Don't criticize your art, and don't get caught up in making it look perfect. You may want to use your image as a catalyst to let your hands and heart produce a different image. There are no rules for how this is done, so let go of any anxieties and give your hands and heart freedom to create. (Allow at least 20 minutes for this portion of the exercise.)
- Look at what you created. Does it surprise you? How did this visualization come to you? Was it an image in your imagination? Did you simply sense what it might look like? How is it related to your intention? What was it like to pray in this way? Where did you feel God's presence most deeply? Where did you feel most distant from God?
- Close with a short prayer of gratitude for the many ways God is present with us in prayer.

Tips

Create a collection of your favorite art supplies to keep on hand for this prayer.

If you feel creatively stuck, get up and stretch or move around. Stop and take some deep breaths as well.

Chapter 5

DISCERNMENT PROCESSES

O NE OF the questions most frequently asked of pastors, spiritual directors, and pastoral counselors is, *How do I know what God is asking of me in any given situation?* It's the question at the heart of Christian spiritual discernment. The bad news is that we can never be completely sure—even when we think we are. God is Divine Mystery and we must not ever think we have Divine Mystery by the tail. The good news is that Christians have asked this question for centuries and some of our ancestors in the faith have left for us some excellent guidelines and helps for discerning God's will in any given situation.

What exactly is discernment? In popular parlance, it is used to refer to thoughtful decision making. But that's only part of what we do when we live a life of Christian spiritual discernment. Notice I said "live a life" not "do a task." Surely we can put our life questions to a series of processes to attempt to determine where God is leading. But true discernment is not so clear-cut. Wilkie Au, professor of spirituality at Loyola Marymount University, says holistic discernment is "a process of experiential learning in which we discover the ways of the Spirit in our lives over time," and he emphasizes that it is "personal and idiosyncratic, not formulaic."[1]

Christian spiritual discernment is listening to the Holy Spirit's movement in our thoughts, emotions, and bodily reactions and then using that information to weigh and sift possibilities as we make choices in alignment with the Spirit. That's my definition. It begs the question, *What constitutes listening to the Spirit?*

71

In her book on discernment, Debra Farrington speaks of spiritual discernment as "hearing with the heart."[2] Thomas Green calls it "discovering in prayer how God wishes us to act."[3] David Lonsdale calls it "listening to the music of the Spirit." These phrases are poetic because discernment is art, not science. You learn to discern as you listen to your thoughts, emotions, and body in any given situation, looking for those places where "fruit of the Spirit" (love, joy, peace, gentleness, goodness, faith, meekness, temperance) is evident. And good fruit takes time to form on the tree.

True discernment is always done in hindsight. We pray, listen, evaluate, sift through possibilities, and then we act—-only finding the fruit of the Spirit later. Discernment is not finished when we make a decision. We only determine our best assessment of God's will after we seek confirmation of that decision, asking ourselves and God, "Was that, in fact, where you were leading?" If you are seeking absolute certainty about a decision by working through a discernment process, you are likely to be disappointed. But if you are longing to be in deeper relationship with God by working with God, on a trial-and-error basis, to make faithful choices, then you are likely to find Christian spiritual discernment meaningful.

In this chapter, I will offer you three prayer-infused processes that you may use to help discern God's direction in your life in any given situation. There is no need to follow any particular process slavishly. The genius is not in the steps, but in discovering which elements of the process unlock for you a greater understanding of how God lives and moves and breathes in your life.

Most of all, discernment is an adventure. Trust that God meets you where you are and will take you where you need to go on this adventure.

Ignatian Spiritual Discernment

In Christian spiritual discernment the goal is to hear God's voice in the midst of the many voices in our lives calling us here and there. Early Christians were implored to "test the spirits to see whether they are from God" (1 John 4:1). Ignatius of Loyola (sixteenth century) found that discovering God's will in a person's life was a matter of mind, body, and spirit. By using the Ignatian examen over time (see chapter 4), we can begin to see where God speaks most actively in our hearts through myriad positive feelings that encourage, support, and affirm what seems right to us— Ignatius called this "consolation." We also begin to see where we run into negative feelings that discourage, disturb, or call into doubt our choices—this he called "desolation." Both of these are what Ignatius calls movements of the heart and are indicators of God's guidance. That is why practicing the examen over a long period of time is helpful in everyday discernment.

But our consolation and desolation need to be considered alongside our capacity to think things through rationally as well, especially when facing serious crossroads in life. The process presented here will help you consider all of what you know about how God moves in your life as you make a choice.

You can find many books on Ignatian discernment, and each one will translate his methods and concepts a little differently. They all will emphasize a few key elements, which are included in this process and highlighted in italics. The Ignatian approach is well rounded and well tested over time. It provides a general roadmap for that adventure we call discernment.

However you use this, do not feel compelled to answer all these questions in one sitting. Discernment takes time. Important questions may take months to discern. Each time you return to the process, be sure to spend time in the first two steps—*preparation* and *desire to follow God's leading and indifference to all else*—before moving on.

Intention

To seek God's desire for us in a given, concrete life situation.

The Exercise

- *Prepare.* Find a quiet place where you will not be disturbed as you enter this adventure with God. Have a journal on hand to write your reflections or jot down your thoughts. Light a candle and begin this process with a prayer, asking God to open your mind and heart to God's desires. Ask for honesty of heart, and inner freedom from any destructive habits.

- *Desire to follow God's leading and be indifferent to all else.* Ask God to help you become indifferent to anything that is not of God. This does not mean you are uninterested in the outcome of your discernment, but it means you are willing to leave the outcome in God's hands. If you feel you cannot find in yourself this place of "holy indifference" to the outcome, then express to God your desire to be open to God's leading, saying something like, "Lord, help my lack of indifference."

- *Frame the question.* Name the issue you wish to discern. It should be a concrete and concise question. Questions that are most helpful are those that can be answered yes or no (as in "Should I start to look for another job?") or those for which you can list realistic and concrete choices. Your question may change over time in discernment. Write out your question and sit with it in prayer. Pay attention to any insight, emotion, or felt body sense that arises in you.

- *Look at the question rationally.* First, list two or three choices that would answer your question. Make a list of pros and cons for each choice. Gauge at this point which choice you are leaning toward. How does each choice feel after considering the pros and cons? Weigh your lists. Which pros and which cons feel more important than the others? Make a tentative choice before moving on to the next step.

- *Look at your life situation.* The tentative choice you made will affect the context of your life. How will this decision affect your family? Your lifestyle? How is your circle of friends affected? How does the choice fit into your personal spiritual journey? What image of God pervades as you consider this issue? What is the background history of the issue under consideration? What are the facts at hand? Now that you have spent some time with this choice, hold it in the light of your desire to follow God. Notice how free or unfree you feel as you imagine yourself pursuing this choice. At this time, do you want to go back and consider other choices? If so, do that now and proceed with a new tentative decision.

- *Look at your beliefs and values.* When you think about your choice, how are your personal and spiritual values honored? What "fruit of the Spirit" (Galatians 5:22) is evident? Is the choice in accord with the biblical witness? Does this choice increase your generosity, openness to others who are different, your self-esteem? Does this choice allow you to love as Jesus loved?

- *Listen to your intuition.* Imagine your thoughts dropping down into the center of your being and becoming very still. Listen to your breath for a few minutes. Now, allow any images to emerge freely for you. Does any image predominate? In what way does this image relate to your choice? What is your gut feeling about the path you have chosen? As you ponder your options, what is your present body language? How does your body feel? Can you identify a felt sense within your body that is related to this choice? After listening to your intuition and to any images or bodily senses that emerged, do any new ideas or choices emerge?

- *Use your imagination.* Imagine yourself living out the choice you are most leaning toward at the moment. Then, imagine taking a different course. Which feels more right? More free? In which choice did your body feel relaxed and energized?

  Imagine that you are very old and looking back on this decision. What will you wish you had done?

  Imagine that your best friend came to you with a similar question and was leaning toward a similar choice. What would you advise?

  Imagine that you are explaining your decision to the wisest person you know. What do you imagine they would say to you?

- *Examine your consolation and desolation.* As you continue to test the option you are leaning toward, examine it to see if you are feeling more consolation or desolation:

  Consolation. A mostly positive movement of the heart (even in the midst of grief or longing); an increase in faith, hope, and love; inner and lasting peace; joy; an inner knowing that encourages, supports, and enlivens your decision. Consolation generally draws you closer to God.

  Desolation. A mostly negative movement of the heart (even in the midst of good fortune or excitement); a turning away from faith; a restlessness, heaviness, or anxiety; an inner knowing that discourages, calls into doubt, or dulls the energy around your decision. Desolation generally makes you feel far from God.

- *Make your decision.* Based on all you have experienced in the questions and tests of this process, make a decision. Notice your immediate reaction. Is it one of consolation or desolation? You may choose not to act on the decision right away, testing to see if your feelings and thoughts remain the same for a few days. At some point, though, you must act on faith on the decision you have made.
- *Test the decision.* How does the decision feel after taking action on it? Do you have the energy to live it out? Are you feeling more consolation or desolation? Does your decision fit with the law of love that Jesus calls us to? How have the people in your life responded to the decision? What "fruit of the Spirit" (Gal. 5:22) have you noticed? Do you feel closer to God or farther from God as a result of taking action on your decision? If, after testing the decision, you believe it not to be a call from God, do not panic. This is a time for ongoing discernment. Do you need to adjust your decision?

Tips

If you find it too daunting to approach this process alone, consult a spiritual director or a friend who is wise and discerning. If you want to stay with specifically Ignatian-style discernment, find a Jesuit or Jesuit-trained spiritual director. Catholic retreat centers in your area can help you find the right person.

Discernment doesn't have to follow a long, complex process. If you have a relatively easy question in your life that you want to decide with God, look over this process and see which questions are most helpful. Answer those and pray with those. The process is meant to be a guide and a help, not a hindrance. Make sure, though, that you follow the first two steps every time you approach God in discernment. They are the foundation of Christian spiritual discernment.

Quaker Clearness Committee

Another way of Christian spiritual discernment is a Quaker model that involves individuals asking trusted, wise, and spiritually grounded people in their lives to help them discern. Known as convening a "clearness committee," this process is infused with silent prayer while the trusted friends gently ask the person seeking "clearness" some simple questions prompted by the Holy Spirit.

The process is simple, but for many of us it will not be easy. It requires far more listening than speaking, praying than probing; and a close attention to what is real, what is important, and what is holy. Historically, Quakers used clearness committees to help couples in their local meeting (the Quaker term for congregation) discern their desire to be married to one another. Parker Palmer describes the practice of a clearness committee:

Each of us has an inner, divine light that gives us the guidance we need but is often obscured by sundry forms of inner and outer interference. The function of the clearness committee is not to give advice or alter and "fix" people but to help people remove obstacles and discover the divine assistance that is within.[4]

Naturally, a clearness committee works more smoothly if everyone on it has experienced one. But not all of us have that luxury. The process of clearness committee is worth following, even if it feels awkward at first. As long as everyone involved knows and accepts his or her role, follows the guidelines, and agrees to approach this as a prayerful time of exploration, it should be a helpful experience for the person in need of discernment.

Clearness committee may also be used by a group in need of discerning a matter as a group. Guidelines for that are found in the Leader's Guide at the end of this book. The process listed here is for an individual "focus person" who wants to convene a clearness committee for discernment.

Each clearness committee session includes a time toward the end of the process for assessing whether spiritual consensus has been achieved. This does not mean that everyone is in full agreement on every point. It does mean that the group has a sense of the direction in which the Holy Spirit is leading. If the group does not, another meeting may be held with some time in-between for individuals to pray. Or, it may mean that some people in the clearness committee are holding on to agendas that they want to promote rather than submit to the leading of the Holy Spirit. Again, prayer and openness to God's preferred outcome are called for. Consensus is never about bullying or waiting for everyone to relent and be agreeable. It's about listening to the Spirit and doing the best you can to determine in which direction the Spirit seems to be blowing.

Intention

Discovering and accepting the divine assistance within as we struggle with a question.

The Exercise

Setting the Stage

- Everyone in a clearness committee needs to understand the roles and responsibilities:
  1. **Focus person.** This is the person seeking clearness on a question or challenge in his or her life. It could also be a couple. The focus person writes a short summary (one to two pages) of the situation to be discerned, with a concrete question about the situation noted at the top of the paper. This paper is then distributed to each person he or she has asked to be a discerner. The focus person arranges the time and place for the discernment.
  2. **Discerners.** These are the people whom the focus person has chosen to help with discernment. They need to understand that they are primarily on hand to listen to the situation and question at hand, to pray, to keep silence, and, when they feel so led in their prayer, to ask *simple, direct questions* designed to help the focus person listen to the divine assistance within. Discerners agree to follow the guidelines listed below.

3. **Clerk.** This is one of the discerners who agrees to keep time and make sure the guidelines are being followed.

- Everyone in the clearness committee needs to understand the guidelines:
  1. Discerners and the clerk are at the service of the focus person. If, at any time, the focus person does not want to answer a question, then you are not to press the focus person.
  2. Discerners are only to ask simple, honest, and caring questions. The questions should not include statements, prefaced remarks, or stories. A question should never be advice or judgment cloaked in the form of a question. It will be up to the clerk to intercede gently and ask that a question be reframed if it does not meet this guideline.
  3. Discerners should not, in any way, try to "fix" the focus person, give advice, or "set them straight" about anything.
  4. Discerners should take care that their questions are prompted by their prayer insights or the urging of the Spirit and not simply their curiosity.
  5. Discerners need to be mindful of the need for silence between questions and after the focus person has answered.
  6. The discerners do not give their opinion on anything—including consensus—unless asked by the clerk at the appointed time or by the focus person in the short time for questions of the discerners, at the end.
  7. All that is experienced in the clearness committee is to remain confidential. Only the focus person has the freedom to share what they experienced afterward. If the focus person asks a discerner for more information, then the discerner may answer. But the discerner is not to approach the focus person to say more, ask more, or reflect more on the matter.

The Process

- The focus person chooses three to six people as discerners and invites them to participate in this process. The focus person asks one of them to be the clerk, who will keep the time and enforce the guidelines. The focus person finds a date and place and sets aside at least two hours for the clearness committee meeting.

- The focus person writes his or her short explanation paper of the situation under discernment and distributes it to the discerners well before the meeting gets underway.

- *When it is time for the meeting to begin,* the clerk begins by going over the guidelines to make sure everyone understands their role and responsibilities. Then, the clerk will open with a period of silence (at least 10 minutes). The clerk will signal when the silence is done and ask the focus person to begin with a summary of the situation or question.

- When the focus person has finished his or her summary, the clerk will ask for a few more minutes of silence. When that is done, the clerk opens the floor for *simple, direct, and Spirit-prompted* questions from discerners.

- The clerk will ask for times of silence if the pace of the committee seems too fast. Ideally, silence will surround each question and answer, giving discerners and the focus person space to think, feel, and experience God's promptings.

- At the end of one hour, the clerk may choose to offer a silent stretching break of five minutes.

- At the end of ninety minutes, the clerk will ask the focus person if he or she has a sense that the Spirit is moving in a particular direction. The focus person may elaborate. The clerk then asks the discerners if they experience consensus. They are merely to indicate if they think the answer to the question about consensus is yes or no. They are not to discuss the heart of the matter, at least not at this time.

- The clerk will ask the focus person if he or she, at this time, has questions for any of the discerners. The discerners are to keep their answers relatively brief and confined to the focus person's questions. If the focus person wants to talk about consensus (or lack thereof), he or she should bring it up. If the focus person does not bring it up, discerners need to keep silence on the matter.

- At the two-hour point, the clerk will ask the focus person if he or she would like another clearness committee on this situation or question. The focus person may answer or may want time to think about it. If the focus person is sure that he or she wants another session, arrangements may be made for that following the close of the session.
- The clerk closes the committee time with prayer and reminds discerners of their commitment to confidentiality. The discerners turn their copies of the focus person's paper back to the focus person.

Tips

Read more about what Quaker educator Parker Palmer has to say about clearness committee in his book *A Hidden Wholeness: The Journey Toward an Undivided Life* (Jossey Bass, 2004). See the chapter on "Living the Questions" (pp. 129-49).

If you feel you need the kind of help that clearness committee offers but cannot convene a group of three to six people, consult a spiritual director, show that person the guidelines for clearness committee, and ask that the person use the Quaker concept of simple, direct, and Spirit-led questions to help you discern. Alternatively, find a trusted friend and go through the process with that friend as your sole discerner. (Make sure you share the guidelines with that person!)

The Wesleyan Quadrilateral

John Wesley, one of the founders of Methodism in the late eighteenth century, was a preacher, theologian, and deeply spiritual person. What has come to be known as his "quadrilateral" was based on four factors that he believed illuminated Christian life: Scripture, tradition, reason, and experience.[5] Wesley didn't create this as a discernment process or leave a method—what I present here is a process based on the quadrilateral, an excellent guide for considering important matters.

Visually, the quadrilateral looks like this:

Scripture   Tradition

Reason   Experience

Though you will find disagreement about whether these four factors should be considered equally (many Protestants insist that Scripture holds more weight than, say, tradition), what is not in dispute is the necessity to test our discernment questions in all four areas. If you go back and check the Ignatian discernment method, you will find all four factors are woven into the fabric of that discernment in some way.

The beauty of the Wesleyan quadrilateral is that it is easy to remember and visualize, so you don't have to find a lengthy method to follow when you have something you want to discern. After using this process a few times, you will have the main questions memorized and you can put your life questions to the test quite easily.

As with all the other discernment processes, it is important that you enter by abandoning your fixation on any particular outcome (seeking what Ignatius calls "holy indifference") and turn your attention to what God is calling you to be or do. If that seems too difficult, then ask God for the desire to live out God's purpose in this discernment.

Intention

To explore God's will through consulting Scripture, tradition, reason, and experience.

The Exercise

- Begin with a clear understanding of the question or issue to be discerned. Write the question down so you can refer back to it.

- Enter an attitude of prayer. Sit in silence with a breath prayer or sacred word for several minutes. Release the tension in your body.
- Ask God to be especially present to you as you consider the four points of the quadrilateral. Ask for God's direction in your life.
- *Scripture.* Consider your discernment question. What, if anything, does Scripture have to say about the question? One way to do this is to consider the theme of the question. Can you name the theme in biblical language? Then, look that word up in a concordance. Think also of biblical stories that may allude to your situation. What guidance does God's word have for you in this matter?
- *Tradition.* What does the history of Christianity have to say about your question? What do the famous Christian creeds or statements of belief have to say? How have Christians in the past made similar decisions? What do your trusted spiritual friends have to say about the question? If you have a spiritual director, what is his or her response to your question?
- *Reason.* What do your intellect and capacity for reason have to offer in this question? What is the most logical course of action? What in this matter do you know to be true and not true? List the pros and cons of all the options you have in this question.
- *Experience.* Based on your past experience of living out your Christian faith, how are you feeling led to act in this matter? Where is God's presence most deeply felt when you consider this question? What direction are you leaning? What is your gut feeling?
- After putting your discernment question to all four points of the quadrilateral, reflect on which point was most helpful for you. Which point seemed the most difficult? How are you feeling about the question? Does an answer emerge?
- Stay in silence for a few moments as all this discerning sinks in. Which option or answer to your question most warms your heart? Which answer provides a deep sense of peace or interior joy? Which one feels most right?

- Make a preliminary choice in the matter. Consider in silence how that choice feels to you. When you feel ready, act on that choice, giving thanks in prayer to God for guidance.
- Some time after taking action based on this discernment, return to prayer and test the decision. Has living it out produced "fruit of the Spirit" (Galatians 5:22)? Do you need to spend more time in any one point of the quadrilateral? Does the choice need to be revised or updated?

Tips

Draw the quadrilateral on a sheet of paper and do this discernment visually. It will help you see which point you gravitate to most naturally.

You may want to stretch out this process over time, stopping to research what your tradition says about certain matters at hand or to mine the Scriptures for wisdom.

Chapter 6

BODY PRAYERS

T IS easy in our busy lives to begin to think that we "have" bodies rather than that we "are" bodies. All of our experience of God is filtered through some aspect of our bodies—usually involving our mind at some point. It makes perfect sense, then, to acknowledge and intentionally include our bodies in prayer.

Presbyterian theologian Craig Dykstra once observed that "you can know things on your knees that you can't know sitting in a chair."[1] When we engage our bodies in prayer, we experience God in new ways. This is especially true for people who are what multiple-intelligences scholars call "body smart," possessing a lot of bodily-kinesthetic intelligence. But even if we are not body smart, we can know different things about God as we move in different ways.

As people who grew up with the benefits of the Enlightenment, in which the mind was given priority, it is not always easy to do as the Orthodox mystics suggest and allow our minds to sink deep into our body's center and pray with movement, senses, and breath. If you are a head-oriented person, these prayers may feel awkward to you at first. You may want to say, "But I'm not a dancer or even very knowledgeable about movement." That's okay.

These prayers are not designed to have you move in difficult or uncomfortable ways. All they do is call attention to the role of your body in communication with God. Forget about how you look or even how different these prayers are from your daily style of prayer. Focus only on being in the presence of God and using your body in all the different ways we pray—thanksgiving, praise, supplication, silence, or lament.

It is not uncommon for some people to reconnect with God in a powerful way as a result of body prayers. I once met a woman who had grown disillusioned with prayer until she attended a retreat where she was taught some simple body prayers. What she needed was to *feel* communication with God—in a variety of muscles—not just in her brain.

As you stretch, breathe, and walk your prayers, notice how your relationship with God stretches, breathes, and walks as well.

Breath Prayer

In Jewish and Christian thought, breath is closely related to Spirit. The Hebrew word *ruach* means "breath," "spirit," or "wind," and we first encounter it in the Bible as the "wind from God swept over the face of the waters" as the earth was being formed (Genesis 1:2). This multifaceted word points to breath as both a life-sustaining action for humans and a God-infused action in creation. A breath prayer is one that moves in and out on the wind of your breath, as the Spirit of God intermingles with your own spirit. It reminds us of the time the resurrected Jesus breathed on his disciples, saying, "Receive the Holy Spirit" (John 20:22).

This is a wordless and imageless prayer that involves more being than doing. You are simply observing and following your breath. As you breathe, your body, mind, and spirit are enlivened by God's Spirit.

Intention

To follow breath as it leads to God.

The Exercise

- Find a comfortable position to sit in for at least twenty minutes. Make sure you will not be distracted by telephones or interruptions during this time. If you think you are likely to lose track of time, set a timer or alarm clock to chime when your prayer time is up.

- Express to God your longing to experience God in this prayer. Then, let go of expectations and simply breathe. Exhale slowly, allowing each breath to find its own rhythm. Breathe through your nose unless there is some reason you cannot do so.
- Focus your attention either on your inhalation or exhalation. Feel the breath moving across your nostrils and entering your lungs.
- If your attention wanders, bring it back to your breath. Seek relaxed yet focused awareness.
- When your time in prayer has come to a close, express your gratitude to God for the breath of life.

Tip

As with centering prayer, the steps here are simple, but the practice of them is not always easy. It may take some time before you find this prayer soothing. Over time, your ability to focus on your breath will most likely increase. But even when you are struggling, know that God—who is Spirit—is with you in the breath of the prayer.

Focusing Prayer

How many times have you felt, deep within your gut, what you needed to do? The field of biospirituality—pioneered in our time by Fathers Edwin McMahon and Peter Campbell—champions this body wisdom and gives us helpful techniques for listening to it.

As suggested before, there is no religious experience that is not filtered in some way through our bodies. When we say we feel a sense of God's presence, we are saying that something deep within our body is resonating with something holy. Yet, throughout the history of Christianity, there has been a suspicion of the flesh. Biospirituality workshop leader the Reverend Marjorie Hoyer Smith explains, "Jesus came to reconcile us to God, to show us how to live *in the flesh* as bio-spiritual creatures. In Christ we are made new and whole, empowered to fulfill God's purposes *in the flesh*."[2]

So, as new creatures in Christ, we embrace our body's wisdom. One way to do that is to practice this focusing prayer, popularized by McMahon and Campbell and based on a biophysical method that was created by philosophy professor Eugene Gendlin for listening to places within our bodies that hurt physically, emotionally, or spiritually.[3] The prayer involves some creative visualization and imagination, so relax and get ready for something completely different in prayer.

Intention

Experiencing God's Spirit in our body's felt senses.

The Exercise

- Find a comfortable place to be still and quiet for twenty to forty minutes. Begin by asking God to be present to you in your body and your felt senses.
- You will be asking yourself a series of questions. You may write your responses down, but if writing feels like a distraction, do not interrupt the exercise to write.
- Focusing steps:

  Close your eyes and breathe. Let your awareness settle to the center of your body. What do you feel there?

  What location or part of your body wants your awareness right now? (Spend time allowing this to emerge.) Is there an important feeling in your body that needs listening to right now?

  Communicate with this felt sense in your body. Tell it, "I'm here. I'm listening." Ask this bodily feeling if it's all right to go further.

  What is the best way to describe this felt sense or sensation in your body? Is there an image that emerges? If it helps, give it a name (such as "tight neck" or "lump in the throat").

Sit with this body awareness without judgment. Simply observe. Does this bodily sense have an emotional quality? What is the emotional quality?

Ask, "What makes me feel _____ (name the emotion)?"

Ask the sensation what it needs.

Ask your body to show you how healing would feel.

You may want to put your hand on that part of the body and send it warmth. Also, if you feel so moved, ask Jesus, God, or the Holy Spirit to help you care for this part of yourself. Gently end your conversation with the felt sense. Thank your body and its senses for being with you in this prayer.

- End by writing in a journal about what this bodily sense has to say to you about your life. Where do you feel God's healing touch most deeply? How is it to pray in this way? How is it to listen to your body?
- Thank God for being present in this prayer. If you learn something about yourself that needs to be applied in your life, commit yourself to an action that honors the prayer.

Tip

As you use this prayer on a regular basis—and especially when you have a strong felt sense around an emotionally charged situation—you will find the gift within it. You will begin to notice how incredibly knowing your body is, and you will learn to listen when it speaks, and long before it has to scream at you in pain.

Praying with Beads

The Catholic Rosary is the most well known form of praying with beads, but it is not the only form. With the Rosary, a series of memorized prayers are said for each bead along the string with times of reflection on the mystery of salvation found in Jesus Christ.

For this prayer you may use a Rosary or you may purchase or create a set of beads (any length will do) for your own use. The beads are physical reminders to pray, either certain memorized prayers or a prayer of the heart that you use regularly. As your fingers touch a bead, you say a prayer.

The order of prayers listed here is simply a suggestion. Feel free to designate your own prayers or prayer method for your beads. There are as many ways to pray with beads as there are beads and people in the world.

Intention

To communicate with God using beads as holy reminders.

The Exercise

- Select or create a string of smooth, round beads of any length to hold as you pray. Keep a Bible close if you need to read the words of some of these prayers. Spend a few moments in silence at the end of each prayer, pondering the mystery of faith.
- Touch the first bead and recite the opening of the Gospel of John (John 1:1, "In the beginning was the Word, and the Word was with God, and the Word was God").
- Touch the next bead and recite the Lord's Prayer (Matthew 6:9-13).
- Touch the next bead and recite the Beatitudes (Luke 6:20-31).
- Touch the next bead and say the Jesus Prayer (Jesus Christ, Son of God, have mercy on me).
- Touch the next bead and recite the doxology ("Praise God from whom all blessings flow; Praise God all creatures here below; Praise God above ye heavenly hosts; Creator, Christ, and Holy Ghost").
- You may repeat the five prayers in the same order or repeat one of them over and over until you have fingered all your beads.
- Close with the doxology.

Tips

The prayer listed here is not the rosary. If you want to experience praying the Roman Catholic rosary, visit the Web site of the Rosary Confraternity of the Catholic Church (www.rosary-center.org) for specific instructions on the traditional prayer. There is also an ecumenical group that has created a rosary based on Jesus' miracles (www.ecumenicalrosary.org) and a Web site with a rosary specifically for Protestants (www.christianrosary.com).

Make your own bead prayer by creating a string of beads of any length you want. Assign to each bead your favorite prayer or Scripture. Ten beads could represent the Ten Commandments. If you enjoy reciting Christian creeds, assign a bead for each creed. Mix and match as you desire. A full rosary or a small ring of wooden beads with a cross can be purchased at Catholic bookstores, and Eastern religion prayer-bead bracelets are available at many gift shops and bookstores.

Prayer Walk

Mindful walking is a devotional practice in many religions. It is prayer in motion, walking calmly and confidently with an openness to God's revelation. It differs from your daily power walk in that you are not setting a goal. You are not trying to walk faster, longer, or more vigorously. You are not trying to get somewhere. You are just walking in the light of God's love, listening to the gentle rhythm of your breathing, your stride, your heartbeat.

Intention

Taking a step-by-step walk with God.

The Exercise

- Decide where you will walk.
- Begin the walk with only one intention—to experience God in the walking. Express that intention to God and ask for God's grace along the walk.

91

- Ask God to use the walk to communicate something to you.
- Keep your senses open to any sight, sound, smell, or taste that you may experience. Be open and accepting but do not be anxious for this experience. Let it unfold.
- Listen to your breath as you walk slowly. How many steps are you taking per breath? Just observe. Do not control.
- Listen to your heartbeat.
- Listen to the sound of your footsteps.
- Listen to the environment around you.
- If you have a prayer of the heart that you want to recite, say one half on inhalation and the other on exhalation. For example: "Lord in your grace" (inhale), "Grant your peace" (exhale). Repeat this along the walk.
- When your walk is finished, stretch your arms toward heaven and say a prayer of gratitude for mobility, breath, and life.
- If you wish, you may write in a journal about this experience at the end. What was it like to pray in this way? Where did you experience God's grace along the walk? Where did you feel God communicating with you? What did you notice? What part of the prayer was easiest for you? What part was most difficult?

Tips

You may want to read more about mindful walking from Buddhist monk Thich Nhat Hanh. His book *The Miracle of Mindfulness* (Boston: Beacon, 1996) would be a good place to start.

While engaging in this prayer, if you are enjoying the awareness that comes from simply listening, watching, and soaking in the environment, feel free to skip the step in which you begin to say a word prayer.

Praying the Labyrinth

One of the most popular prayer walks for Christians today is the labyrinth. A labyrinth is an ancient prayer practice involving a winding path that leads ultimately to a center and then winds back out to the point where it began. It is not difficult to walk—there are no dead ends as in a maze. The path is symbolic of the journey inward toward God's illumination and then outward, grounded in God and empowered to act in the world.

Much has been written about the labyrinth and the traditional three-fold mystical path of *purgation, illumination,* and *union,* which the labyrinth's paths and center can symbolize. There are many ways to approach this prayer walk—I have outlined only one here. For much more on this fascinating prayer exercise, see *Walking a Sacred Path* by Lauren Artress (New York: Riverhead, 1996).

Most people choose to walk this prayer slowly, but everyone's pace will differ. Some people even crawl or dance the labyrinth. If you encounter someone on the labyrinth and want to go around them, by all means do so gently and graciously.

Intention

To walk a symbolic path that brings you closer to God.

The Exercise

- Locate a labyrinth. You can find permanent ones in many locations (see tips below), and some organizations own temporary ones that can be put on the floor. A finger labyrinth, either drawn on paper or carved in wood, works well if you cannot walk or if there is no labyrinth nearby.[4]
- Pause at the opening of the labyrinth. Ask God to walk with you and to help you through the stages of prayer.
- *Purgation.* The winding path leading to the center allows you time to release all that is within you that distracts you from God. Empty yourself and let go of a need to control your life. Practice this purgation all the way to the center.
- *Illumination.* The center is a place to stop and be fully present to the moment in God. Sit, kneel, or stand in the center for prayer and meditation as long as you like. Be with God in any way you desire—through silent or worded prayers.
- *Union.* The winding path leading away from the center allows

you time to integrate any insight you received in prayer. Walk this path with gratitude.

- Pause at the end of the labyrinth, which is also where you began this journey. Thank God for being with you, both in this prayer and in the life journey that it symbolizes.

- Whenever you are ready, reflect on your experience. You may want to write in your journal. What happens when you pray in this way? What was the time of purgation like for you? Illumination? Union? Where did you feel God's presence most abundantly? How is walking the labyrinth different from other forms of prayer that you enjoy? How is it similar? How is walking the labyrinth a symbol for your spiritual journey?

Tips

Some churches have permanent labyrinths in their court-yards. Check the Web sites or call local Episcopal and Catholic churches. (They seem to be leaders in the use of labyrinths.) Also check the online "labyrinth locator" provided by Veriditas, an organization founded by the Reverend Lauren Artress (http://wwll.veriditas.labyrinthsociety.org).

If you have no labyrinth and want to walk this prayer, an alternative is to meander in and out of the pews of a church, with the front of the church as the center. Return by winding in and around the pews on the opposite side of the church. Another alternative is to create a walking loop for yourself in your neighborhood and designate the top of the loop as the "center." Practice purgation as you approach the center, illumination in the center, and union as you return from the center.

Some additional ways to pray with a labyrinth include taking a life question in as you pray and noticing how God addresses your question; repeating a phrase or word (mantra) throughout the walk; pouring out your heart and asking for help as you walk. Or you can do the prayer walk method of simple aware-ness throughout the exercise.

Embodying Scripture

Frequently we read Scripture and even pray from it, but how often do we *embody* Scripture? By "embody" I mean simply allowing your body to move as you read or hear a biblical story.

In this exercise, you will be asked to form body shapes or prayer postures based on the story of Naomi and Ruth moving to Moab. This is only one of many stories in the Bible that lends itself to movement. You could also move to the parable of the Good Samaritan (Luke 10:25-37), the Prodigal Son (Luke 15:11-32), or any of the colorful stories in the Hebrew Scriptures. You might also want to try a variety of prayer postures as you say the Lord's Prayer.

Try this out and notice what you know while moving that you didn't know while sitting down.

Intention

To experience God's presence in body movement.

The Exercise

- Begin by asking God to be present to you in your body and motion as you encounter God's word.
- Read Ruth 1:1-22 slowly. Imagine being with Naomi and her daughters-in-law as this scene unfolds.
- Reread verses 15-17, beginning with Naomi imploring Ruth to go back to her people and Ruth's poetic reply.
- Place your Bible where you can refer back to it, and find a comfortable place to move around.
- Read verse 15 and embody the words "back to her people." You may move to this phrase in any way you desire. Stay with this phrase for a few moments.
- Read verse 16a and embody the words "Do not press me to leave you." Pause in silence.
- Read verse 16b and embody Ruth's words "Where you go, I will go." Pause.

- Read verse 16c and embody Ruth's words "Your God [is] my God." Stay with this prayer posture a bit longer. Allow it to shift or change if need be.
- Read verse 18 and embody what Naomi understood in the words "determined to go with her." Pause in silence.
- Embody Naomi's stance and what she may have felt as you read the phrase "She said no more to her."
- End with a final prayer posture of gratitude to God for the gift of God's word in the story of Naomi and Ruth.
- Write in a journal about this prayer experience. What is it like for you to pray in motion? In what way is expressing yourself to God in movement easy for you? In what way is it difficult for you? In what way is this prayer different for you? Which phrase is most meaningful to you? Why? What physical responses did you have to the story? What were you able to know in movement that you didn't know about the story before?

Tip

Try this exercise at home alone if you are self-conscious about moving in prayer. This is not an exercise in dancing or "pretty posing"; let your body guide you in the movement. Don't think about your stances too much. Just let it flow.

Confession Body Prayer

A common pattern in the Christian life is to confess our sins and shortcomings before God, only to return to guilt and remorse at a later date. This prayer of confession can help us embody our confession in a way that helps our body let go of the hurt and shame. The movements are a way to physically mark our words and own our confession.

This is a simple prayer, used by the Alternative Worship Collective of Thornbury Methodist Church in Bradford, UK, that is easy to remember and powerful in practice.

Intention

To confess our sins before God in movement.

The Exercise

- Make fists. In your mind's eye, put all that comes between you and God—all your sin and brokenness—in your clenched hands.
- Open your hands and offer these shortcomings to God. Allow God to forgive you.
- Cup your hands to receive God's blessings.
- Place your palms together in front of your heart in a traditional prayer pose as you express your gratitude to God.
- Repeat as often as you like.

Tip

For more resources from the Alternative Worship Collective, see their Web site at www.btmc.org.uk/altworship/collective.htm.

Chapter 7

PRAYERS OF THE IMAGINATION

ENTERING PRAYER with the mind's eye is a creative way to be in relationship with God. Ours is such a visual culture, feeding our imaginations with vivid images and memories. We can cultivate our imaginations through guided meditations, visualization exercises, even daydreams.

Sports psychologists know that if they can help their clients visualize a strong performance, then that is more likely to become reality. Choosing to ponder the variety of outcomes in any given situation can prepare us for what comes our way. Envisioning and focusing on positive outcomes prepares us to seek a blessing, just as envisioning and focusing solely on a negative outcome prepares us to look for a curse. Which do you want to be ready for in life?

The prayers in this section that ask you to visualize desire are not mere wish fulfillment. You will not be attempting to conjure any magic solution. You will, however, be cultivating patience and trust in God. The psalmist says, "Take delight in the LORD, / and he will give you the desires of your heart" (Psalm 37:4). Our first task is to delight in God, and as we come into alignment with God's desires, we can trust that God fulfills our own deepest desires.

We begin with a practice from the sixteenth-century Ignatian *Spiritual Exercises* in which we place ourselves—via our imaginations—in a situation in the life of Christ. In this initial exercise, be aware of how active your imagination already is when you encounter Scripture; then, during the prayer, let your imagination run free. The other prayer exercises involve discovering within yourself the desire for God, for the world, for your communities, and for your life. You will then take these desires in some way into prayer and express them to God.

At the heart of these exercises is the faith that planted within us are God's desires to be fulfilled. Rather than seeking shallow human desires such as the accumulation of material wealth or power over people, our task is to find those desires that produce the fruit of the Spirit.

Ignatian Imagination Prayer

Within the *Spiritual Exercises* of Ignatius of Loyola is the practice of entering a scene out of Scripture that involves the life, death, or resurrection of Jesus. If you have done a few of the biblical reflections in chapter 1, you will find this practice quite familiar.

In this exercise you will use your imagination and the application of all your senses to ponder the story, ending with a colloquy (which means "dialogue") with a character from the story. You will close with a recitation of the Lord's Prayer.

This exercise is adapted for the nativity scene, but you may choose any story from the Gospels for the imagination prayer. You may, of course, also choose any story in the Hebrew Scriptures. Feel free to use this imagination prayer with *any* meaningful text. In fact, in my book *Meeting God in Virtual Reality: Using Spiritual Practices with Media* (Nashville: Abingdon, 2004) there is a method for using this prayer with media clips.

Intention

To imagine that you are physically present in a scene of Jesus' life and to allow that scene to become prayer for you.

The Exercise

- Begin with a preparatory prayer asking God for the grace that all your intentions, actions, and imaginings be used in the service and praise of God.

- Read Luke 2:1-15 (the birth of Jesus). On the first reading, simply take in the details of the story. Pause in silence. Then read it a second time, slowly, allowing your mind to visualize the flight to Bethlehem, a pregnant Mary, shepherds, and angels. Let a visual depiction of this story develop in your mind.

- With your mind's eye, see the road from Nazareth to Bethlehem. How long is it? How wide? Is it bumpy or smooth? Dusty or muddy? See Mary and Joseph going over hills and valleys. Join the caravan. Notice as they stop at the cave or stable where the manger is. How big is this room or enclosure? How small? How low or high? How is it furnished? Where are you in the scene? What part do you play in the unfolding events?

- What sounds do you hear in the manger area? What are Mary and Joseph saying? As you stand nearby, what are you saying? Does anyone speak to you? What is your reply? What sounds other than voices do you hear? Are the animals quiet or noisy?

- What are the smells of the manger? Linger a moment and imagine what you are smelling as you stand near the holy family.

- Is there a taste you associate with the scene? Linger a moment and notice what, if anything, your taste buds reveal about the scene.

- In your imagination, move around the scene and touch various people, places, and things. Touch Mary, Joseph, and the baby Jesus. Touch an angel or a shepherd, if they are present in your scene. Touch the walls of the "cave," the hide of an animal. Notice what sensations you experience as you imagine touching someone or something in the scene.

- Let your full imagination run free at the close of the story. Allow the scene to change in any way you feel inspired. Imagine what more there is to the story than what is recorded in Scripture. Linger and interact with the characters there. What are you doing? Do you go off to tell someone about your experience? How do you describe what happened?

- When you feel finished with the imagination exercise, think about the meaning of the birth of Jesus for your life. Consider the way Jesus was born—in a cave or stable to a poor family. What does this mean for you? What part of the story warms your heart most? What part of the story disturbs you most? What insight does your imagination prayer provide?

• Engage in dialogue with one of the characters in the story. Do this in your imagination or on paper, whichever is easiest for you.

• Conclude with the Lord's Prayer.

Tips

If this prayer is meaningful for you, continue through the book of Luke, taking one scene at a time from the life of Jesus and applying the same kinds of questions.

For those interested in reading the original *Spiritual Exercises* of Ignatius, take a look at *Ignatius of Loyola: Spiritual Exercises and Selected Works* in the Classics of Western Spirituality series (Paulist Press, 1991). For a more modern and gender-neutral version of the *Spiritual Exercises,* see *The Spiritual Exercises Reclaimed: Uncovering Liberating Possibilities for Women,* by Katherine Dyckman, Mary Garvin, and Elizabeth Liebert (Paulist Press, 2001). Many other adaptations of the exercises exist and can be found in libraries or bookstores nationwide.

Wall of Prayer

The Reverend Daniel Wolpert, a spiritual director and Presbyterian pastor, uses this prayer to help individuals and groups better envision their hopes and desires in prayer. Described in his book *Creating a Life with God* (Upper Room, 2004), this exercise marries the creativity of writing with the visual arts.[1]

Do this exercise over time, and you will create a wall for expressing your prayer to God in writing or drawing as well as a place of remembrance to review and savor your past prayers.

Intention

To create a wall where all your longings and desires are expressed to God.

The Exercise

- Obtain a poster board or large piece of thick newsprint to represent your wall. You may place it on the ground or tape it to a wall. Collect pens, pencils, crayons, markers, or other writing, drawing, or painting materials you want to use.
- Begin in silence, marking the time as prayer. Light a candle or say a short word prayer, inviting the light of Christ to be present as you search and express your deepest desires before God.
- At the top of the wall, write the question for this prayer, which is: "When I think from my deepest and truest self, what is it that I most desire from God?" Spend a few moments in silence on that question.
- When you are ready, begin to write, draw, doodle, or paint your feelings and expressions to God around that question on your wall of prayer. Stay as long as you like, expressing yourself on the wall. When you are finished for the time being, say a closing prayer.
- Each time you express yourself on your wall of prayer, fill in a different area.
- When your wall feels full, spend some time reflecting on what you see. What do you notice about your wall? What is at the heart of your desires? What do you feel is God's response to your wall? If you want, record something of God's responses on your wall.
- Leave your wall up so you can return to it at any time. Over time, as a desire is fulfilled or perhaps falls away, note that on your wall as well.

Tips

You may want to invite friends to add their prayers to the wall. Explain the question to them and offer them a marker or pen. See how their desires mesh with your own.

Don't worry too much about whether your desires are pure enough or good enough. God has a way of transforming our lesser desires and pointing us to deeper ones. If any of your desires seem frivolous but real, ask yourself, "What's the deeper desire *behind* this desire?"

Desire Prayer

This is one of my favorite prayers because it allows me to get my desires before God openly, unabashedly, and with feeling. That's because when you pray, you use all your senses to create—in your imagination—a scene that depicts what you desire, and you pray *in* and *through* that desire.

It may sound a little New Age, but the prayer is really quite "Old Age" in that this adaptation comes from prayers handed down by our Native American and Celtic ancestors.

I first discovered this type of prayer in *The Isaiah Effect,* a book by Gregg Braden. He calls it "David's Prayer," named after a Native American friend who introduced him to the idea of surrounding yourself with your deepest desire and offering it to the Creator. In David's prayer, David is in the drought-ridden desert Southwest and he intends to, as he puts it, "pray rain."[2] Not pray *for* rain, but to enter into a way of prayer in which his gratitude for all of creation leads him to feel, touch, taste, smell, and see what he believes the land needs most—rain. After doing that, David leaves the outcome up to the Creator. Braden, a student of quantum physics, contends that aligning ourselves, in gratitude, with our most fervent desire and then deeply feeling what it is like to have the desire fulfilled, can catalyze change in the world.

In a Celtic version of this prayer, found in Tanis Helliwell's *Take Your Soul to Work*, you do much the same.[3] And again, you leave the outcome to God. Helliwell adds an important step, though. You ask God how you might assist in fulfilling this desire, and you watch for opportunities to present themselves.

I've combined and adapted these prayers to keep the emphasis on God's action in the world, and our cooperation with the action.

Intention

To pray our desires before God.

The Exercise

- Begin by taking a few moments to become calm. Say a prayer of gratitude for all that has been, all that is, and all that will be in your life.
- Let your heart's deepest desire be stated before God. Take a few moments in silence to see if the desire remains the same or if you want to state it in a different way.
- Visualize your desire. Feel it. Touch it. Taste it. Smell it. Let it become real to you in your imagination. Linger there and see how the scene depicting your desire develops or changes. *Stay with this step for several minutes.*
- Let go of specific outcomes. Ask that God's desire be fulfilled in your desire, or that God will transform your desire as needed. Notice what, if anything, changes as a result of that request.
- Ask God how you might assist in fulfilling this desire. Stay in silence as you allow space for God to speak in and through your imagination.
- Close by thanking God for this desire and for the opportunity to pray in and through it. Thank God for being present in this prayer.
- Spend a few moments right after the prayer reflecting on how it was to pray with a desire. What surprised you? Moved you? Inspired you? What disturbed you? How did you feel God's presence in the midst of this prayer? Did anything about your desire change as you prayed it?

- In the days following this prayer, be aware of ways God may be offering you opportunities to live into the desire. When opportunities appear, take prayerful action and don't forget to thank God for the opportunities and eyes to see them.

Tips

It is easy to get caught up in our desires and become overly self-concerned. This prayer helps us let go of our desires because we hand them over to God. Use this prayer when you have a desire that persists and feels important.

Remember Psalm 37:4: "Take delight in the LORD, and he will give you the desires of your heart." Ponder what that means before you begin this prayer and make sure you focus just as much on "delighting in the Lord" as you do on receiving "the desires of your heart."

Chapter 8

REFLECTIONS ON MEDIA

W E LIVE in a media-saturated culture. Each day thousands of promotional messages clamor for our attention. Television has become our national storyteller, with the TV screen becoming a focal point in most of our family rooms.

What has prayer got to do with our media culture? Everything. Even if you were to "kill your television" and attempt to ban all brand-name advertising from entering your home, your life would still be heavily influenced by media. That's because the rest of us have *not* attempted to remove ourselves completely from the media culture, and we are your neighbors, friends, and coworkers. So the influence seeps in.

Some of us find great meaning in the stories of popular culture. Some have even felt the Spirit of God move in and among us as a result of a story we saw portrayed in film or television or as we watched a news event unfold before us on television.

This chapter is for all of us—those who push against the media culture and those who are open to its influence. In these exercises, you will be looking at media in a prayerful way. Like all our other exercises, you'll begin each one with the intention of opening yourself to God's Spirit, and in the midst of the exercise you'll be using awareness skills to analyze, interpret, and draw meaning from these visual "texts." Remember that the producers of these visual stories are people, like you, on a spiritual journey. Their creativity and imagination, like yours, are gifts from God. When you use media in prayer, you are allowing their gifts to be a window to the Divine.

Analyzing Pop Culture Texts

Within Christianity, the spiritual discipline of study or analysis has historically been important. Think about how preachers prayerfully study a biblical text and other books in order to prepare a sermon. You'll be looking at media in much the same prayerful way.

This prayer bonds the mind with the heart as we approach visual texts (usually film or television clips) in search of theological meaning. The method presented here is adapted from a longer version found in a book I coauthored in 2001, *Watching What We Watch: Primetime Television Through the Lens of Faith* (Geneva Press). It's a series of questions used in media literacy—that is, the application of critical inquiry to all aspects of media. It is in the consideration of these questions that we find the theological message of any media text emerging.

Use this method anytime you see a scene from film or television that moves you or piques your theological interest. As you pray and study, allow God's presence to infuse all that you do.

Intention

To reflect on the theological messages in visual texts.

The Exercise

- Before you start this prayer, decide on a short media clip—from a film, television show, or video—that you will reflect upon. (For our purposes, this clip will be referred to as a text since you will analyze it as you might a written text.) Have it cued up and ready to go. If you prefer to write down your reflections, have a journal handy.
- Begin by turning your attention to God. Take several deep, slow breaths. Ask God to be in your analysis and in the asking of the questions.

- Play your chosen media clip.

  Think about the genre. What kind of film, TV show, or video is this?

  What previous texts might it remind you of?

  What was going on in the world at the time this text was created?

  Who does the targeted audience for this text seem to be? How do you know that?

- Play the media clip again.

  What is the ultimate concern portrayed here?

  Is genuine perspective introduced? If so, in what way?

  Is anyone being left out here? What would their perspective have to offer about the ultimate concern?

  How does our experience of God or the way we talk about God answer the questions raised by the text's ultimate concern? What does our faith tradition have to say about it?

  In what way does this text support or undermine your religious beliefs?

- What do you know about this media clip now that you have analyzed it that you didn't know before? What surprises you? What moves you? What disturbs you?

- Ask God to be present to you in the analysis of this clip. How is God revealed as we search for ultimate concerns in media? Take a few moments of silence to answer that question.

- Close by saying a few words of gratitude for those who create meaningful media and for the way God can use it to speak in our lives.

Tips

Keep the clip short. If you are using a clip from a television show, choose one that seems heavy with meaning and isolate the important scene only. If you are doing this alone, you will have watched the show beforehand and know the context. If you are using this with a group, you may have to set up the scene with a few words about the context.

You may need to do this exercise a few times before you begin to get a feel for many of the nuances involved in film and television production. For visual nuances, try watching the clip without sound and simply viewing the visuals. For the nuances in writing and presentation, close your eyes and listen to the clip without watching the visuals. These ways of isolating the components of a visual text can help you in the analysis process.

For more information about considering a media text for analysis, the Center for Media Literacy in Los Angeles has an excellent Web site with many resources available online. I especially recommend the free orientation guide from the CML MediaLit Kit. Find it at www.medialit.org.

Images of God in Media

God is popular these days in film and television. God has been portrayed as the Force in *Star Wars* films, in the faces of old and young people in *Joan of Arcadia,* and as a folksy janitor in *Bruce Almighty.*

Not all images of God are created equal. Some will resonate with you and others may leave you puzzled or disturbed. In this exercise, you will consider the image of God that is being portrayed on screen and how you respond to it.

Although this is another analytical exercise, surround it with prayer and you will find the tone of the exercise to be more mindful.

Intention

To prayerfully consider images of God seen in visual texts.

The Exercise

- Before you settle in for a time of silence, select a film or television clip that in some way either portrays God, alludes to an image of God, or visually presents an aspect of religion or spirituality. Have the clip ready to play.
- Take a few moments to breathe and settle into silent prayer. Then, ask God to be present in the viewing of the clip and in your questions. Ask God to reveal whatever you need to have revealed.
- Watch the clip. Then, rewind and watch it again.
- What is the image of God suggested here?

  For help on this, examine both the dialogue *and* the religious symbolism.

  How are the characters in the clip responding to this image of God?
- How does this image of God fit (or not fit) with your own? Think about both your chosen images of God and images you grew up with.

  If the image in the clip appeals to you but is not one you usually think of for God, how might this image help in the development of your relationship with God?

  If the image in the clip repels you, think about why that is. Is it a non-biblical image? Is it an image that doesn't fit with the loving and merciful nature of God? What is disturbing you about this image?
- What is your response in prayer to the image of God presented here? What do you want to say to God about this image? What might God be trying to say to you in the midst of this reflection?
- Close by letting go of all visual images of God and simply sitting in the presence of the Divine Mystery we call God.

Tips

If you need help finding a clip for this exercise, consider any of the following:

- A clip from the CBS-TV drama *Joan of Arcadia* in which Joan talks with God.
- A scene from *Bruce Almighty* in which Bruce encounters God.
- A clip from any of the *Star Wars* films pertaining to the Force.
- The scene in *American Beauty* where Ricky shows his girl-friend the "dancing bag in the wind" video.
- A scene from any of the *Oh God!* films.
- A scene from *The Apostle* in which Sonny prays aloud to God.

Keep in mind that the clip doesn't have to have a physical representation of God. Clips of people talking about God, praying, or characters exhibiting deep spiritual motivations are all excellent texts for this exercise. Videotape some of your favorite shows as you watch them and begin to notice how often some image of God shows up. You may also find, from time to time, commercials that depict religious images or spirituality.

"God" on Prayer

Since God is such a popular character onscreen, it is worthwhile to see what the film or TV representations of God have to say about prayer. Granted this is more an exercise in what producers of film or TV shows about God *think* God has to say about prayer, but it highlights some ideas that people in our culture harbor about how God communicates with us.

You will need to view one or more of these films or TV shows for this exercise: *Dogma, Bruce Almighty, Oh God!* or *Joan of Arcadia.* You may be able to think of others in which God was played by a human being.

This will end up being a prayer—about images of prayer. Be open to learning more about your own theology around prayer as you evaluate these popular culture images.

Intention

To reflect on a media portrayal of God and how God communicates with us.

The Exercise

- Watch the entire film or television episode on tape at home prior to this exercise. Make a note of where a scene about prayer is found.
- Begin with a time of silence. Then, ask God to increase your understanding of prayer as you reflect on these media images.
- Replay your selected scene from a film or television show in which God communicates in some way with humans. Be especially mindful of dialogue, images, or situations that contain a message about how God communicates with human beings. You may want to watch the clip twice.
- What attitude does this onscreen God take toward our prayers or our attempts at communication? Describe the attitude and how you came to that conclusion.
- How does this onscreen God respond to prayers or human requests?
- How do you think God responds to our prayers? What is an answer to prayer?
- How does your understanding of God's response to humans compare with what you saw in the clip?
- Express now to God your feelings and thoughts about how God responds to prayer.
- Allow a time of silence in case God wants to respond to what you just expressed. Wait for a felt sense of God's presence.
- Close by thanking God for mercy and grace toward humans in our many needs.

Tip

To expand this exercise, use a Bible and a concordance (listing of passages by subject) and look up a variety of passages on prayer to see what the Bible has to say about God's response to our prayers.

Strong feelings may emerge as you consider your beliefs about prayer. For example, some people feel great sadness over a prayer they think was not answered. Allow yourself to be fully present to whatever emotion you feel rather than discarding it because you think you should not feel that way.

Meditation on *The Apostle*

Many film critics call Robert Duvall's film *The Apostle* the best religious film ever made. It takes seriously the heartfelt faith of the protagonist while also portraying his human flaws without flinching.

The Christian faith teaches that we are born into a broken world in which good and evil coexist. *The Apostle* depicts Sonny's struggle with a dual nature. In this film, Sonny (Duvall), the Southern Pentecostal preacher, attempts to remain faithful in the midst of this struggle between his God-centered nature and his homicidal temper.

For this exercise, view *The Apostle* in its entirety at home. Then write in a journal using the questions listed in the prayer exercise.

Intention

To explore the movements of the heart while reflecting on *The Apostle*.

The Exercise

- Begin in prayer, asking God to be present and active as you watch and reflect on this film. Spend a few moments in silence before starting the film.

- Watch the film with a journal and pen nearby. Note places in the film where you feel your heart is moved, inspired, surprised, or disturbed.
- After viewing the film, write in a journal on these questions, continuing to note where you feel particularly moved in some way:

  What is the evil that Sonny struggles with?

  Would you characterize Sonny as basically a good man who did a bad thing, or a bad man who talks about God a lot? Or would your characterization defy categories of good and bad?

  When Sonny is shown shouting his prayer at God in his bedroom, what image of God do you think is being portrayed? How does Sonny's image of God compare with your own? What does the image of God in *The Apostle* seem to say about how humans are to relate to God?

  Film critic Roger Ebert says *The Apostle* "escapes convention" and "penetrates the heart of rare characters." What do you think he means by escaping convention? Can you think of other films that treated the subject of Pentecostal preachers differently? What about the treatment of preachers or ministers in general—what are some conventions (widely accepted devices or techniques) used in films to portray ministers? Also, what do you think made the portrayal of Sonny so "rare," as Ebert puts it? If you agree that Sonny's character was rare for a film portrayal, what do you think was the message being sent by the rare portrayal?

- Go back to your journal and see where you were particularly moved in the film. Which scenes rang spiritually true for you? Which scenes did not?
- In silent prayer, reenter the one place in the film where you most felt your heart warmed or inspired. Ask God to use that scene to speak to you. Wait for any felt senses of God's presence.
- End by talking aloud to God—much as Sonny did in his bedroom that night—and pouring your heart out in prayer.

Tip

You can find *The Apostle* in most public libraries and video rental stores. Much has also been written about producer, director, and actor Robert Duvall's years-long effort to get this film made.

Meditation on *Entertaining Angels*

How do we live out the love that Christ has called us to? An excellent film for exploring this question is *Entertaining Angels: The Dorothy Day Story*. Dorothy Day was a Catholic laywoman (1897–1980) who became a leader in the Catholic Worker Movement. She cared for and served indigent and homeless people, keeping Christ's commandment to love one another as her highest goal.

There is a scene in this film in which the Cardinal of New York questions Dorothy's stance on social issues, and confronts her out of concern that people are calling her a communist. In this short exercise, you will reflect on that scene and what it has to offer your life.

Intention

To reflect on what love calls us to by pondering a scene from Dorothy Day's story.

The Exercise

- Begin with silent, centering prayer using the Jesus Prayer ("Jesus Christ, Son of God, have mercy on us") as your sacred phrase. Return to the Jesus Prayer when your mind wanders. Do this for ten minutes.
- Ask the light of Christ to illuminate your heart as you watch this film.
- Watch *Entertaining Angels* in its entirety. Make note of which scenes touch you most deeply. When the film has ended, review your notes. What happened in those scenes? How did they

relate to your life right now? In what way was God particularly active for you in the watching of those scenes?

- Return to the scene where the Cardinal of New York confronts Dorothy. Watch it again.

  What is this scene saying about how we are to live as Christians?

  What is this scene saying about how we are to be "church" for others?[1]

- Now return to your notes and see which scenes touched you most deeply.
- After watching this film, where do you feel Christ is calling you to be more loving and compassionate in the world?
- Close the way you began, with the Jesus Prayer.

Tip

Much has been written by Dorothy Day and about her life and ministry. For her biography, check out Robert Coles's *Dorothy Day: A Radical Devotion* (Perseus Books, 1989) or Jim Forest's *Love Is the Measure: A Biography of Dorothy Day* (Orbis, 1994). For writings by Dorothy Day, begin with *Loaves and Fishes* (Orbis, 1997).

Where Is the Faith?

Within any story there is an embedded theology—that is, a way of speaking about "ultimate concern." Faith shows up, in some form, in almost every film or television story—maybe not faith in God, but faith in someone or something.

In this exercise, any film or television story will suffice. The goal is to seek out and answer the question, "Where is the faith?" As you use this exercise repeatedly, you will begin to see how theology is woven into all stories.

We all have faith in something. It's important to understand that and then be intentional about where we place our faith.

Intention

To ponder where the faith is in any given visual text.

The Exercise

- Choose any film, television, or video story. Have it ready to watch.
- Begin with a breath prayer using the phrase, "My faith is in you, O God (Christ or Spirit)." On the inhalation silently say the first part of the phrase, and on the exhalation say the name you have chosen for God. Do this for at least five minutes.
- Watch your chosen visual text. Focus on one specific character, looking for what this character is putting faith in.
- Where does this character's faith reside? In what does he or she ultimately trust? How do you know that?
- What do you think the writer or producer is trying to say about the world through this character's faith?
- Where is this character's faith placed when compared with the placement of your faith?
- What is God revealing to you about faith in this story?
- End with the same breath prayer that you began the exercise with: "My faith is in you, O God."

Tips

Place a sticky note on your television set with the question, "Where is the faith?" It will remind you to reflect on this question repeatedly.

During prime time one week, watch several of the most popular television shows with the question "Where is the faith?" in mind. Notice what or who many of the characters place their faith in.

You're the Producer

As you may have noticed, many visual stories tell truths about God without explicitly mentioning God, Jesus, or the Holy Spirit.

There are many reasons for this, the main one being that producers want their stories to have universal appeal. As you reflect on media in prayerful and mindful ways, you will notice many ways producers express what we as Christians might call "fruit of the Spirit" (Galatians 5:22) in the context of their stories. Using a variety of symbols and metaphors, producers create rich stories full of meaning and religious values.

How would *you* present concepts such as compassion, confession, reconciliation, resurrection, or liberation in a story that has universal appeal? That is the question at the heart of this reflection.

Intention

To contemplate how you might present Christian values in a media story.

The Exercise

- Before starting, find five blank index cards. Place one of the following words at the top of each card: compassion, confession, reconciliation, resurrection, liberation.
- Begin in prayer, offering yourself to God and asking God to be present in your imagination and creativity.
- Take time with each card. Imagine you are a film or television producer. For each card, think about how you might—as a producer—depict the concept written at the top of the card *without using any explicit religious or biblical imagery or language.* Think of a storyline or scene that would tell a story of compassion, confession, reconciliation, resurrection, or liberation. If you feel creatively blocked in coming up with a story, think about stories you've seen before that illustrated those concepts.
- When you are finished writing, go back over your cards and read what you wrote.
- How easy or difficult is it to illustrate these concepts without using explicit religious language or images?
- Which cards were the easiest to write? Which ones were more difficult?

- Would you enjoy being a producer and having to make these kinds of creative decisions? Why or why not?
- Where, in this exercise, did you feel your creativity flowing most freely? Where did you feel your creativity blocked?
- In what way have you felt God's presence in the midst of this exercise?
- Close with a prayer of gratitude for creative artists who find ways to speak truths about God even when they do not use religious language or images.

Tip

If you find index cards to be too confining, you may do this exercise in a journal or use full sheets of paper.

Chapter 9

PRAYING FOR OTHERS

N O DOUBT in many of the prayers presented in this book, you have been praying for others, since our highest calling is to love, care for, and pray for one another. But the prayers in this chapter are designed especially for those situations in which we want God's loving touch to be felt in the world.

It's popular in Christian circles to say that prayer works. Yet no one knows *how* prayer works or what exactly constitutes an answer to the many requests we make of God on behalf of our families, friends, and loved ones. It's a matter of faith. We pray because we trust that God precedes us in caring about all aspects of human life. We pray because we know prayer changes how we think, feel, and act. And sometimes we pray because we don't know what else to do—we've exhausted all human action on behalf of the one we are praying for. We have no choice but to leave the concern in God's hands.

Praying for others not only involves petitions for our loved ones, but also prayers for the larger human community—our neighborhoods, churches, nation, national leaders, and the world. Praying for others sometimes means praying *with* others at their request.

Praying for others does not have to involve petitions or requests of God. Sometimes we have no idea what the person or situation *needs* from God, but we know they need something. So we pray with an open heart asking that God's desire for that person or situation be fulfilled. In doing this we follow Jesus, who taught his disciples to pray, "Your will be done." At the center of this prayer is a deep trust that God's will involves whatever is best for the person or the situation—even if the outcome is not what we would have chosen.

In most churches there is a time during worship for prayers of joy and concern, and it's a wonderful communal time of praying for others. In this chapter, I want to show you a few other ways to approach God on behalf of others—ways that I hope will help increase your appreciation and practice of praying for others.

Intercessory Prayer

With intercessory prayer you are praying on behalf of another person. This is a popular form of prayer, especially for church groups and within worship.

I once participated in a prayer group that met once a week at a church to pray for others. After many weeks of speaking our requests out loud, some in the group felt that they wanted to try something different. So, I introduced them to an "imaging intercession," which I found in Marjorie Thompson's best-seller *Soul Feast* and have adapted here for you.[1] We found that to combine imaging with our heartfelt spoken requests was powerful.

Intention

To communicate with God our deepest hopes and desires for others.

The Exercise

- Begin seated comfortably in a chair. Take at least five deep, slow breaths. Allow your thoughts to slowly descend deep into the center of your being. Say to yourself, "Here I am in the presence of God's everlasting care and love."
- Using words, either spoken or unspoken, state who and what you are praying for. Let your prayer be uncensored. Just lay your heart's desire out before God.

- Then become silent. Allow a visual image of God surrounding the person to emerge in your imagination. It could be a bright light, or Jesus holding the person in his arms, or any image that presents itself to you. In your mind's eye, see the person becoming whole and reconciled in the situation. Feel the grace of God transforming the person or situation.
- Using words, spoken or silent, ask that God's desire and purpose for the person or situation be fulfilled. Release the person or situation into the fullness of God's care. Leave the outcome in God's hands.
- Repeat the process for as many people as you wish to pray for.
- After your final intercession, raise your arms in a body prayer, offering all that you are and all that you prayed to God.

Tips

There are many theological views on intercessory prayer. *Soul Feast* includes eight, with Scriptural references for your consideration (Westminster John Knox, 1995, p. 38).

We naturally want God to answer our prayers in the way we desire. Surrendering to the mystery of God's will takes maturity. If this is difficult for you, remember that it was also difficult for Jesus in the garden of Gethsemane. So you are not alone. Simply acknowledge your difficulty in prayer and ask for courage to pray, "Your will be done."

Healing Prayer

There is no *one way* to pray for healing. I like this prayer because it does not require that we know much of anything at all about the particular situation we are praying for. If you've ever had the experience of wanting healing for yourself or another person, but not knowing what you want God to do, then you know how necessary a prayer like this is.

In this prayer, you simply visualize the person in the light of God's love and healing power. You may also visualize Jesus—the great physician—laying his hands on the subject of your prayer. Rather than using words and petitioning for God's help, in this prayer you are trusting in the certainty of God's loving care and leaving the outcome in God's hands.

Intention

To hold a hurting person or situation in the light of God's love and healing power.

The Exercise

- Begin by lighting a candle as a symbol of the Divine Light.
- State your intention before God: "I am praying for God's healing of _____." Ask God for faith and trust in healing. Ask God for courage to let go of the outcome and to allow God's healing to take any shape or form.
- Visualize a brilliant, warm, shining light from God surrounding you and softening your heart, mind, and body. Bask in this light of the world for a few moments. Let it remain around you as you continue to pray.
- Visualize the warm light expanding and surrounding the person or situation that needs healing. See the light softening and releasing any dysfunction or pain. Feel love and compassion for the person or situation. Stay in prayer with this light for several minutes. In your mind's eye, watch the light as it heals.
- If you have more than one person or situation to pray for, repeat the last step for each one.
- To complete this prayer, visualize the light that surrounded you and each subject of prayer becoming more concentrated and burning brightly in your hearts.
- Close with a prayer of gratitude for the healing that takes place.

Tips

Many Christians have strong beliefs about healing. Some think that if a person is not cured, then healing has not occurred or our faith simply wasn't great enough. Trusting God means letting go of agendas like that. Healing does not always mean a miraculous cure. It does mean that God's presence has transformed the person or situation we prayed about in some way. And, we may not ever be privy to knowing how that transformation manifested itself.

When praying with a person who has asked for a healing prayer, listen carefully to their prayer request and then let them know you will be praying silently, visualizing God's light and healing love surrounding them.

Prayer Partnering

Some people prefer praying for others rather than praying for themselves, so they find a prayer partner and exchange intercessions for one another. This can be done by meeting on a regular basis, either in person or by telephone. Or it can be an informal relationship in which each person informs the other of their prayer requests and the two people pray on their own at different times.

The prayer partnering described here is for a face-to-face meeting. It embodies and relies on what Jesus promised, that "where two or three are gathered in my name, I am there among them" (Matthew 18:20).

Intention

Praying for one another side by side.

The Exercise

- Set a time to meet with a trusted friend who wants to be a prayer partner. Make sure you are in a quiet space and will not be distracted or disturbed. Decide on one person to keep an eye on the time, especially during the times of silence.

- Light a candle as a reminder of Jesus' promise to be in the midst of your partnership.
- Open with a few moments of silence.
- Check in with one another. One at a time, talk about what is going on in your life at this present time. Answer the question, "How is it with your soul today?"
- The first person shares his or her requests for prayer. The listener follows "deep listening" guidelines (see the Deep Listening exercise in chapter 2): remaining silent when the other is speaking; no interrupting or commenting; no fixing, saving, giving advice, or setting one another straight. Allow a few moments of silence after the sharing.
- The listener now moves into the role of praying for (and with) the one who just shared. You may say a prayer aloud or silently based on what the person just shared. If a spoken prayer is offered, allow a few moments of silence before moving to the second person's sharing.
- Now the second person shares his or her requests for prayer. The listener remains silent. Allow a few moments of silence when the sharer finishes.
- The listener then moves into the role of praying for (and with) the one who just shared, either silently or aloud. If words are used, allow for some silence at the end.
- After praying for one another, spend some time in reflection. Where did you feel God's presence most actively? What insights, if any, did you receive in prayer? How did it feel to pray in this way, with a friend? Let your conversation center on where you felt most held by God.
- Close with each person saying a short prayer of thanksgiving that mentions where they felt God was most present.

Tips

Once you get a prayer partnership established with a friend, try some other exercises from this book. Regardless of which exercises you use, move each session into a reflection on where God's presence was most deeply felt.

If you find this type of relationship meaningful, you might want to consider entering spiritual direction with someone who is experienced and gifted in assisting you along your spiritual journey. While spiritual direction is not the same as prayer partnering, it can help you discern where in your life God is most actively at work and thus draw you deeper into relationship with God. To locate a spiritual director, visit www.sdiworld.org and find a listing for the regional director near you. You can also locate a retreat center near you and ask for referrals in your area.

Franciscan Prayer

Francis of Assisi (thirteenth century) never set out to found an order. He simply wanted to restore an old church in his town and to live as Jesus did—as a wandering preacher with as few material possessions as possible. Amazingly, people began to emulate Francis, and the Order of Friars Minor, which we now call the Franciscans, was created.

I suspect part of the attraction to Francis was his style of prayer. He offered short prayers throughout the day—whenever his inner spirit was moved. For Francis, simple acts of loving service were infused with prayer. This is not to say Francis never sat down for long periods of prayer or contemplation, just that what we have come to know as Franciscan spirituality is marked by "free-flowing, spontaneous, informal praising, and loving dialogue with God."[2]

This exercise is adapted from the chapter on "Franciscan Prayer" in *Prayer and Temperament: Different Prayer Forms for Different Personality Types*, by Chester P. Michael and Marie C.

Norrisey (Charlottesville, Va.: Open Door, 1991). In this book, Michael and Norrisey provide prayer practices based on the Myers-Briggs Type Indicator. They write that Franciscan "spontaneous prayer" is especially suited for the SP or "sensing, perceiving" temperament.

Everyone—regardless of temperament—can enjoy this exercise. It's easy and filled with joy.

Intention

To be moved in spontaneous prayer for another.

The Exercise

- Decide on one daily activity involving others that you will use as your prayer. It could be a walk, time with your pet, a phone conversation, a task at work that you enjoy, or time in worship.
- Enter that activity with a short prayer of gratitude. Ask God to move your heart in prayer throughout the activity.
- As you proceed with the activity, be aware of times when your heart is moved. When this happens, offer a spontaneous silent prayer.
- Think of the other people (or creatures) involved in your activity and notice something of God's goodness and mercy in them. As you are moved, offer a spontaneous silent prayer for the person (or creature).
- Ask yourself, "What in this exercise helps me better appreciate God's activity in the world?"
- Be especially aware of the joy that you find in this activity and this person or persons. As you notice the joy, radiate that joy back to God in a silent, wordless way.
- When the activity ends, reflect on how this prayer felt for you. How was it not to stop and pray but to keep going and praying at the same time? Is this how you pray naturally? Where did you feel the presence of God most deeply? How did interaction with the other person change as a result of your spontaneous prayer?
- If you so desire, write about this prayer in a journal.

• Close with a short final prayer. Be silent for a few moments and see what prayer forms in your heart.

Tips

This style of prayer is wonderful for people who feel they just don't have time in their day to set aside for a long prayer or meditation. It is also good for people who are relatively new to the life of prayer.

For those who want more, there are fifteen suggestions for Franciscan prayer in *Prayer and Temperament,* along with an explanation of Franciscan spirituality.

For an educational and visually interesting presentation on the life of Saint Francis, I recommend the video *Reluctant Saint: Francis of Assisi* (2003) filmed on location in Italy. This docudrama is based on the biography of Saint Francis by Donald Spoto, with Robert Sean Leonard providing the voice of Saint Francis and additional narration by Liev Schreiber.

Prayer for the World

The world is such a big place with so many needs; how do we pray for them all? Disciples of Christ pastor and spirituality teacher Joseph Driskill has come up with a way. In his *Protestant Spiritual Exercises: Theology, History, and Practice* (Harrisburg, Pa.: Morehouse, 1999), he wrote a "Prayer for a New Earth" to "reflect the Protestant belief that God's work occurs in all venues of life."[3]

This adaptation is much shorter than Driskill's version, but it has the same focus—expanding our sense of connection to God's work, not just here on earth but throughout the entire universe.

Intention

To pray for the world.

The Exercise

- Seated comfortably, begin by noticing your breath. Take several deep, slow breaths and then just let your breathing return to its natural pace.

- As you rest in God's presence, ask the Holy Spirit to pray in and through you in this reflection. Then, relax and enter the following visualization.

- First, visualize where you live. What are some of the concerns you have at home? Where do you experience God's grace, mercy, and love in your home? Visualize everyone you live with. Ask God to show you how to be more receptive to God's desires at home.

- Now visualize where you work. See your coworkers, your supervisor, and perhaps those you supervise. What issues or concerns are foremost at work? Where is justice, compassion, and hope at work? Do you sense God's activity in any of these issues or concerns? Ask God to show you how to be more receptive to God's desires at work.

- Turn your attention now to your community. Visualize your neighborhood, city, state, or region—any part of it you feel drawn to. What are some of the major issues and concerns for your community? What do you think God wants for this community? How is that being lived out? Is there anything you feel particularly called by God to do in the community? Ask God to show you how to be more receptive to God's desires in your community.

- Visualize your nation or continent. What are some of the most important concerns for this larger geographic area? How might God be working in these concerns? Where is justice or compassion hardest at work? Ask God to show you how to be more receptive to God's desires for your nation or continent.

- In your mind's eye, visualize planet Earth. Where is God's love, mercy, and compassion most needed right now? What do you think God desires for the planet? How could you cooperate with God's desires? Ask God to show you this now.

- Now that you have gone from a small circle of concerns to a global perspective, become still and silent inside. Listen quietly for God's voice leading you to whatever action or situation needs your attention. Stay with this time of silence for at least five minutes.
- If you wish to write about this prayer experience, do so now. Reflect on what you felt God was drawing your attention to most acutely. Where, in this prayer, did you feel a sense of God's activity most deeply? Did any new insights about God or God's activity in the world emerge for you?
- End with a short prayer of gratitude for the ways in which God works in the world.

Tips

It may help to jot down notes along the various steps of this prayer. Then, at reflection time you can more easily recall the movements.

Take plenty of silence for each step. This prayer is not designed to be done quickly.

LEADER'S GUIDE

GENERAL PRINCIPLES OF GROUP LEADERSHIP

PERHAPS THE call you feel is to gather people in small groups for spiritual growth and nurturing. Or someone in your church or faith group has asked you to lead the small-group experience. Deep within, you know that leading a group in a spiritual practice is an incredible responsibility, and your desire is for each person in the group to experience the transforming power of the living God. Now, you may wonder, how exactly do I do that?

For starters, let go of any idea that you are creating this experience of the Holy. Your job is more like that of a master gardener—helping others tend the holy ground while acknowledging that God is wholly responsible for the growth. You are the one who teaches ways to water, nourish, and aerate the soil. You also need to assist others in the waiting time between watering the seeds and seeing growth. The greatest task for leaders of small-group experiences in spirituality is to create an atmosphere in which prayer, listening, and discernment of God's voice are nurtured and allowed to grow.

Once you've done that, you need to trust that God desires growth in this group far more than you ever could and that God will work in the lives of these people regardless of how well the small-group experience appears to go. You need to believe and communicate to the group that God is in charge and is lovingly guiding these participants.

You can also trust that the exercises in this book are techniques that group leaders and spiritual directors who came before you have found helpful in creating an atmosphere in which God's life, love, and power are evident. Much depends on everyone involved—the attitudes and receptiveness of the participants, your excitement about the exercises, and your trust in the providence of God.

Key to the success of these exercises is an enthusiastic presentation. If you believe in what you are presenting, others will as well. If an exercise is new and different, and you suspect some resistance will emerge, take a casual "Let's just try this and see what happens" attitude. The more inner freedom you are able to cultivate and express to the group, the better. Try not to be attached to a particular outcome. Express a spirit of experimentation and then truly experiment.

You don't have to be an organizational specialist to lead an excellent small group in spiritual practices. Here are some general principles to keep in mind.

Leadership Style

There are many kinds of small-group leaders. Decide before you start what kind of role you will assume.

Facilitators ease the process along. The word *facilitate* literally means "to make easy." Most facilitators do not participate in the process but nurture the process. This is a role most new leaders of spiritual practices enjoy. It allows them the freedom to observe and assist in the process without feeling pressed to participate at the same time.

Coaches cheer the participants along. Their job is to educate, inspire, and encourage. Coaches usually do not participate in the activity they lead. In sports, coaches work toward a desired outcome; in spirituality, coaches leave that outcome in God's hands. This role is good for extroverts who like motivating people to try new practices. The challenge is to allow the Spirit to blow in whatever way it will without feeling a need to manipulate a desired outcome.

Peer-leaders see themselves as one of the group. They lead and participate at the same time. This is the most egalitarian of the models, which is its draw. But it can be a challenge for the peer-leader to step in and make corrections or observations as needed. Once you step out of the role of participant to make necessary (sometimes hard) observations, you have established a hierarchy. This peer-leadership model is best to use with groups that appreciate firm ground rules and trust one another to adhere to them.

Once you've determined the role that best fits you and the activity you will be leading, you will need to think about simple ways to make everyone in the group feel welcomed, especially at the first meeting. Greet participants at the door with a warm smile. Show them around the room. Let them know you are glad they came. Have snacks available.

Be excited about the session. If you have done your prep work—a critical part of the process, which is described below—then your anxiety about the group activity should be lessened. If you do feel anxious for any reason, acknowledge this to God in prayer and ask God to be in charge. Visualize the session going well. Then, let it go.

Leader Preparation

Know where you are headed. That's not the same as knowing the outcome! It means that you have spent time in prayer asking God to guide this group and that you have carefully selected the activity, figured out the time it will probably take in your group, practiced the activity yourself in your own personal reflection time, and made necessary room arrangements so that the space is conducive to a time of spiritual exploration.

A good rule of thumb is that you will spend about two hours in preparation outside of the group time for every one hour spent with the group:

- 30 minutes in personal prayer, silence, or solitude.
- 60 minutes going over the activity for your own learning purposes. Visualize each element and take notes on what you experience. Decide which opening rituals and relaxation exercises you will use.

- 30 minutes planning details, such as the structure outlined below.

Once you have done your preparatory work and are ready for the group, commit the experience to God. You have done your part to make it work. Now your job is to lead and let God do the rest.

Structure of the Group

Structure is vitally important to the well-being of the group. People may say they prefer unstructured group experiences—until they have one that goes awry. Reasonable and well-thought-out structure allows for inner freedom. For example, Quakers use the highly structured Clearness Committee process that sometimes, for them, even restricts eye contact between the person seeking discernment and the group assisting that person in discernment. To those who have never experienced a Clearness Committee, this may seem extreme. Parker Palmer, a Quaker writer who has experienced the process many times, says once participants get used to it, the practice is liberating for everyone, drawing them "deep into a space that honors and welcomes the soul."[1] That's the kind of group atmosphere you are looking for, isn't it? Simple structure will help you cultivate that.

Some questions that need to be answered are:

- What is the desired size of the group? Conventional wisdom is that the ideal size of a small group is at least 8 people committed to attending regularly. Naturally, some will not be able to make every meeting, which is why eight is a good number—you're likely to have at least six at every meeting. If you have ten or more people attending you might want to consider splitting into two or more smaller groups, depending on the size and acoustics of the room. Let the activity itself determine if you need to split up a larger group. You'll need to use your instincts on this. If the group you are planning is very small—three to five people—be aware that the feel of the group will be much more intimate and the activities may run shorter.

- Is the group designed to meet for a set number of dates and then disband, or will it be open-ended? Many people prefer to commit to groups they know will end at some point.
- When will the group meet? Will the dates be set prior to the first meeting, or will the group members bring calendars and decide on the next date at each meeting? With our busy schedules, most people need the structure of set dates rather than facing the "calendar challenge" at each meeting. Although it means some people may not be able to attend each meeting, it's easier to remember dates and times if they are already set.
- How long will each meeting last? Will there be a fixed closing time or will it "end when it ends"? (Most people prefer a fixed closing time for planning purposes.) You may want to build into your regular meeting times fixed elements, such as check-ins, silent prayer, or singing, to build in familiarity. Most exercises in this book will be flexible enough to fit into at least a two-hour meeting time. Some exercises will be short enough that you might be able to include two in a meeting. Make sure you also allow time for silence between people's responses and between activities. You may want to build in times of silent reflection as well.
- What will the group be called? How will it be advertised in the community? Who is responsible for communications?
- Who is invited? Is it open to all or by invitation only? Although leaving it open is more democratic, sometimes groups trying out new activities and concepts want to do so first by invitation to test the waters.
- Will the leadership remain constant, or will the group share leadership in order to give more members a chance to experience the role of leader? If sharing is the choice, how will the group determine who leads each meeting?
- How will each session be opened and closed? Each activity begins with some kind of establishing prayer or silent time and ends with a closing prayer. If you don't want to use the opening or closing listed for the exercise, then read through the book and find different ones to use. Vary these according to the

group's needs and the pace or tone of the chosen exercise(s). How you open and close is important, so find "bookend" exercises that you will feel comfortable leading.

Many of these questions can be determined either by you, by a core of people composing the heart of the group, or by the full group during the first portion of the initial meeting. In addition, for every exercise in the book, this leader's guide includes additional suggestions for ways to structure the exercise for group use. Following these important suggestions should make the group experience more trustworthy and meaningful.

Space and Room Arrangement

If the Spirit is present, what difference does the physical space make? A great deal, say many experienced retreat and small-group leaders. Pay attention to the way a room feels. Select a room that is big enough for your group but not too big. If the room is too small, people will feel hot and cramped. If the room is too big, the empty space contributes to a vague feeling of vulnerability. Make sure the room is relatively quiet and not prone to interruptions. Many a retreat leader has learned the hard way that if you choose the room next to a working kitchen, you end up competing with many delicious distractions!

Arrange the chairs or couches in a circle that allows enough space for people to walk in between. Circles allow us to see each other's faces and create the feeling that we are all one body. Unless it's necessary for the exercise, avoid sitting around a table—it can make the gathering feel too much like a business meeting.

A small coffee table or end table adorned with a candle or other symbols of the faith in the middle of the circle is a good reminder that God is present and is central to what will be done at the gathering. Many small-group leaders use the lighting of a "Christ candle" as a ritual to mark the opening of the gathering. A bell, tuning fork, or singing bowl can be used to announce that the circle is forming and the attention is shifting from arrival to gathering.

Covenants and Guidelines

Covenants and guidelines also contribute to a higher trust level among group members. Every group is different, so you will need to choose your covenant wordings carefully. Make sure you cover the basics, which include:

- *Everything that takes place in the group is confidential.* What is said in the group stays in the group. It is not repeated to outsiders, nor is it discussed by group members when outside the group. Confidentiality is *imperative* to a group that is sharing deep, personal matters of the Spirit. Group members will feel more comfortable and confident if they trust that they can speak their truth without hearing about it from a third party or being grilled about it by a group member outside of group time.

- *All participants agree to seek God first in these activities.* These groups are not therapy, civic clubs, or even Christian fellowship. They are focused on experiencing God.

- *No fixing, saving, advising, or "setting one another straight."*[2] This is to ensure that everyone feels safe enough to share honestly and openly. Keep in mind that even if a person *asks* for advice or counsel from the group, it is not a good idea to allow the group to get into a "fixing" mode. Simply explain that this group is not the forum for that sort of request or offering.

- *No debating or judging other people's theology.* A small group dedicated to spiritual growth is not the place to argue theology. Debating or judging people's beliefs has a tendency to close off communication among people and with God.

- *No debating or judging other people's spiritual experience.* Again, the act of debating or judging is not conducive to the kind of openheartedness needed to experience God.

- *No speaking for someone else.* Participants need to use "I" statements when commenting (rather than "you," "you people," "they," "those people," or the all-inclusive "we"). In this group, everyone states his or her own feelings and experiences.

139

- *All group members agree to participate appropriately in all activities.* Trust disintegrates when one member of a group refuses to participate and retreats to the role of observer. Frustration develops when one or two people dominate the dialogue or share inappropriately. Not everyone will be able to share at the same level, but all can share in some way that is both right for them and for the group.
- *All participants commit to regular attendance whenever possible.* Clearly not everyone can make every gathering. But participants should commit to make as many of them as possible.

An important but simple structural element that is completely within the group leader's control is to start and end the group on time. Stragglers will learn to arrive promptly (at least we can hope) and those on a schedule are more likely to continue in the group.

Common Challenges

As mentioned earlier, one of your jobs as a leader is to make observations and corrections when necessary. This is easier for some leaders than others, so be aware of your own comfort level regarding confrontation and be prepared to be assertive. Here are some common group dilemmas and well-tested suggestions for coping:

- **One person is dominating the conversation, making dialogue difficult for the others.** When this happens, it is often helpful simply to step in after the dominator makes his or her last remark and say, "I'd like to hear from some of the other members of the group at this time." If the dominator has in some way diverted the process—taken it off course—you may ask something along the lines of "What just happened to the process here?" Remember that if a dominator is causing you discomfort, he or she is probably causing the same discomfort in the group. The group will appreciate your stepping in and bringing the truth to light.
- **One person is fading into the background, rarely sharing or par-**

ticipating. It is not healthy for one person to be a mere observer while others are opening up and sharing. When everyone shares *something*, trust is built. So as a leader you may need to say, "I'd like to hear from _____ on this," or if there is more than one silent type, "I'd like to hear from some of the members of the group who have not yet spoken." That's usually all it takes to get the observer to become a participant.

- **The entire group has somehow veered completely off course from the activity at hand.** If the mood is lighthearted, the leader can say, "Hey, what just happened here?" If the mood is more serious, simply acknowledge the diversion and gently steer the group back to the question or the activity at hand.

Handling Tears

Prayer can evoke powerful emotions. Be prepared for some tears, silent pauses, and deep questions to arise. When emotions surface, consider them to be perfectly normal. When this happens in a small group, it is best not to call undue attention to the person who is emotional. Hand the person a tissue if need be, but don't encourage the group to fixate on the tears or try to make the person feel better. The person may, in fact, be experiencing tears of joy. Just let it be.

Handling Fear and Anxiety

Some people are fearful of unfamiliar spiritual practices—such as using the Bible for inner reflection, guided meditations, and image-less prayer. The fear of encountering the Holy in a new and different exercise is real and understandable. We are human and our knowledge of God is partial and hazy.

When leading a group in one of these prayer practices, mention that it is perfectly normal to experience deep emotions in prayer. Make sure people understand that it is all right to be moved by prayer! Offer to stay after the session if someone has a particular need to talk about the prayer experience. Listen deeply with your heart, offer reassurance that God is with us in our deepest emotions, and ask if the person would like any assistance in finding someone else to discuss this with, such as a spiritual director or trained counselor. Never discount the person's feelings or attempt to give advice or fix the situation; simply listen and show compassion, always remaining calm and reassuring. Keep the person in your prayers.

Sometimes fear arises because, being human, we wonder if what we experience in prayer is of God or of something else. And the truth is, we can never be entirely certain. We can only do our best. Discernment, which we discussed in chapter 5, involves sifting through our experiences to determine what is good, holy, and acceptable to God. It always involves a judgment call. Here are some ways God's people have traditionally determined whether they are listening to and following God in prayer:

- Is the experience in-line with what we know the Bible as a whole reveals about the nature and purpose of God as understood in Jesus? Does it "do justice, and . . . love kindness, and . . . walk humbly with . . . God?" (Micah 6:8).
- Are we listening to our deepest and truest desires? Are we honoring the gifts God has given us? Many times God pulls us toward our call by way of our gifts and desires.
- Are we choosing the path that seems to hold the most life for us and for the world we live in? God implores us to "choose life" (Deuteronomy 30:19). Jesus tells us he came that we might have life and have it more abundantly (John 10:10).
- When we reflect back on the experience, did it produce "fruit of the Spirit" (Galatians 5:22)? Jesus said you will know his followers by their good fruits (Matthew 7:20).
- Have we involved our Christian community in the search to determine God's ways? Jesus assures us that he is present "where two or three are gathered in my name" (Matthew 18:20). Praying together and sharing wisdom is our gift to one another.

Part of spiritual maturity involves trusting that God goes before us in all that we do. God holds us and enfolds us. When we put each exercise in God's hands, and trust that God can and will work through the process, who or what do we really have to fear?

Evaluating Spiritual Growth

Once you've led a group in spiritual practices, you may wonder how to evaluate the work that's been done. There is no check-off sheet for spiritual growth. Our culture puts so much value on measurable outcomes and accountability, but in the realm of spirituality it boils down to an evaluation of the fruits. As described previously, Paul named a few of these important fruits in his letter to the Galatians (5:22-23): love, joy, peace, gentleness, goodness, faith, meekness, and temperance. In short, if the people in your group become more attentive to the ways of Christ, and more Christlike, they are experiencing spiritual growth. A few questions you might ask yourself and the group after several sessions include:

- Do we feel closer to God? In what ways?
- How has our closeness to God made itself manifest in our relationships with people?
- Are we more aware of the needs of the poor, oppressed, and outcast? Are we reaching out to them in hospitality?
- Have we developed a balance between the inner and introspective life and the outer and outward-focused life?
- Are others drawing closer to God as a result of the changes in us? How so?
- Has our image of God changed in any way? Describe the change.

Some people mistakenly assume that spiritual exploration is something that will make a rich and comfortable life even more so. They are then surprised and dismayed when they find that drawing closer to God sometimes causes discomfort, at least for a while. It is not easy to be honest with God, and, when confronted with our own failures and weaknesses, we feel pain and brokenness. That is part of conversion—a turning around to face God—and it happens many times in the life of a person who develops a living and loving relationship with God.

Be aware that the spiritual is in some ways like the physical—there will be growing pains. So when your group experiences discomfort, celebrate! You're growing, and that's a good sign. The pain is not endless, and the healing that comes from having an honest relationship with God leads to *real* comfort and *real* richness in life.

The exercises presented in this book are ones that many retreat leaders, small-group leaders, and spiritual directors have found helpful in listening to and following God. As a group leader, you will need to help the group discern whether the exercises truly are helping individuals and the group as a whole to "choose life." Over time, you and the group will discover where spiritual growth has taken place.

LEADER'S GUIDE TO EACH EXERCISE

In this section, you are given guidelines to help you facilitate each exercise with a group. Exercise preparations for you to do prior to the meeting are found in a section entitled "At Home"; then you will find a section on "Introducing the Exercise"; necessary adaptations for group use are found in "During the Exercise"; and some suggestions for group reflection time are found in "After the Exercise."

The most important activity any leader can do is to experience the prayer exercise before leading it. Almost every exercise is first written for individual at-home use, so before you present any of the exercises to the group, make sure you try the prayer and have at least some firsthand understanding of it. This will make the group feel safer attempting a new exercise, and it ensures that when someone asks you a question about it, you can answer from personal experience. If the exercise requires a group—such as the Quaker Clearness Committee—you may want to gather a group of friends to experience it so that you will have a feel for how the process works.

Groups differ greatly in purpose. Some groups—such as spirituality circles or affinity groups—are primarily a gathering of individuals who want to pray and share life with God together. Other groups—church or nonprofit boards, sessions, committees, or task forces—are quite task-oriented (I refer to these as working groups) and need to function as a whole, making decisions and listening to the call of God as it pertains not to individuals but to the organization. The exercises that best lend themselves to being used with working groups—various forms of the examen, the *lectio divina* on community, and all the discernment processes—will contain information to assist the leader in facilitating the prayer for a community as well.

CHAPTER 1. BIBLICAL REFLECTIONS

Meditation on the Heart's Longing

At home

- Think about how your group is likely to receive this exercise. Although most people will appreciate it, be aware that some people are not accustomed to associating personal longing with an experience of God. They may try to steer conversation toward the historical context of the passage instead of allowing the group to use the passage for personal meditation. Spend time before the gathering thinking about how you will redirect the focus if that happens.

Introducing the exercise

- Encourage everyone to give this exercise a try—even if it feels difficult at first—because there are many ways of making a Scripture passage part of one's life. One way is to imagine that it is speaking directly to you and asking you the important question.

During the exercise

- Keep the pace contemplative by reading slowly and making sure the times of silence are honored.

After the exercise

- Ask participants to share their personal experiences with the passage and with Jesus' question. Reinforce that this is a time to share one's own experience—not comment on what another person has said. (20 minutes)
- Ask participants to share what they noticed about the exercise *as a group*. What seemed to be happening in the group? Did you feel a sense of God's Spirit? If so, how would you describe it? If not, what do you think stood in the way? How did it feel to listen to Scripture in this way? (10 minutes)

- If this is the end of the group time together, close in prayer. If you are moving on to another activity, take a break at this point.

Dialoguing with Scripture

At home

- Choose the passage to be used and make sure there is a table available for those who need a writing surface.

Introducing the exercise

- Ask participants to keep in mind that dialoguing with a biblical character is simply another way to help clarify our own beliefs and find the wisdom God placed in us. It is also a way to allow God's Spirit to work actively in our imaginations. (Some people may find this exercise difficult or uncomfortable, especially if they are not used to imaginative prayer.) Asking for God's presence and guidance prior to beginning is crucial to creating a trusting atmosphere in the group.

During the exercise

- Skip the step in which participants read their dialogues aloud. Instead go directly from the writing time into the reflection questions.

After the exercise

- After everyone has had a chance to talk about their experience dialoguing with a biblical character, bring the focus away from the individuals' experiences to reflect on the experience *for the group as a whole*. What did you notice about your experience as a group with this exercise? Were there any themes or connecting threads that emerged? What was the group spirit during the exercise? (10 minutes)
- End the exercise with a prayer of gratitude for the experience.

Listening to Wisdom

At home

- Consider the makeup of your group. You will need to break your group into dyads (pairs) for the sharing part of the exercise. When in dyads, participants will practice a particular and countercultural kind of listening in which they will be asked *not* to respond verbally to their partner's reflection.
- Keep in mind that if there is an odd number of participants in your group, you will need to participate during dyad breakout.

Introducing the exercise

- Some people will appreciate the exposure to new, extrabiblical texts, and others may be uneasy. Explain that Sirach is one of the books included in the Apocryphal-Deuterocanonical portion of the Bible used by Orthodox and Catholic churches. And since there was no established canon in Jesus' day, Sirach certainly was one of the Jewish books that Jesus considered a holy text in his tradition.
- Ask participants to share what they know about Wisdom literature in the Bible. Can anyone name three Wisdom books? (Proverbs, Job, and Ecclesiastes are the three most famous.) Explain that you will be reading two passages—one from the Apocryphal book of Sirach (a Wisdom book) and one from Matthew. The Matthew passage is based on Wisdom "teachings" from the Hebrew Scriptures. (Allow 5 minutes for discussion.)

During the exercise

- After everyone has had the opportunity to reflect on the passages and the word of instruction individually, ask that one member of each dyad take five minutes apiece to share what he or she reflected on. *The person who is sharing has the floor and the person listening is not to interrupt or verbally respond during that time.* At the end of the first five minutes, announce that it is time for the second person to share. Again, no interrupting or responding. At the end of the ten minutes, after both persons in the dyad have shared, bring everyone back to one circle.

After the exercise

- Ask participants to share what they experienced in hearing and reflecting on the two passages. Which passage did they find most meaningful? What was it like to reflect on a word or words of instruction? Do you generally respond well to receiving instruction from others? What is it like to receive instruction from God or God's word?
- In what way is reflecting on Wisdom literature different from reflecting on a parable of Jesus or a gospel narrative?
- What was your experience of simply listening—and not responding—in your dyad? What was your experience of being listened to? Was any part of this exercise difficult for you?
- End the reflection with a prayer of gratitude to God for the gift of God's wisdom to us.

What Do You Want from God?

At home

- Gather your materials. You'll need a copy of the guided meditation and a Bible in your favorite translation to read aloud for the group. You will need a watch or timer to keep track of the time for each part of the exercise.
- Become as familiar with this Scripture as you can prior to leading the imagination exercise. In your prayer time, explore the question Jesus asks: "What do you want me to do for you?" How does it feel to bare your desires before God? Is it easy for you to be completely honest with God about what you want in life?

Introducing the exercise

- Explain to the group that this will be a guided meditation on the story from Mark 10:35-40, and that you will lead them through this imagination prayer. Tell them you will read the scripture through twice slowly and then lead them in a time of silent personal reflection. If they want to write in a journal during the silence, have them locate their paper and pens at this time.

- There may be some resistance to using imagination in prayer. If so, acknowledge that this may be new to some people and ask them to simply try it. The theological basis for using our imaginations in prayer is that God gave us the gift of imagination and invites us to bring all of our gifts to prayer. Remind group members that there will be time at the end for them to reflect on the exercise and any resistance to it.

During the exercise

- Do not rush the guided meditation. Allow some silence to give people a chance to let their imaginations run free.

After the exercise

- Allow twenty to thirty minutes for discussion, using the questions listed in the exercise, about what it was like to pray with the imagination.
- At the end, reflect on how this felt as a *group* experience. What did the group notice about the sharing at the end? What is it like to be with a group exploring a Scripture in this way? What fruits of the Spirit could be detected in the group's reflections (love, joy, peace, gentleness, goodness, faith, meekness, temperance)?

Stages of the Journey

At home

- This is a writing exercise, so either advise participants ahead of time to bring their writing implements with them or arrange to provide paper and pens for the group.

Introducing the exercise

- Explain that this exercise will focus on the stages of the Israelites' exodus journey—from the time in Egypt to their arrival in the promised land. Can participants list, from memory, those stages? Which stage seems to predominate in their memories?

During the exercise

- Keep a timer on hand and move participants along the stages of the journey in a timely fashion. Allow five to ten minutes per stage.

After the exercise

- Ask the group to reflect on what they've heard from those who described their journeys. In what ways were the journeys similar? In what ways were the journeys different? How can we assist one another along the various stages of our journeys? What was the role of the spiritual community in the journey? How can we assist our spiritual communities in their various stages of journey with God?
- Thank the group for their reflections. Close the gathering with a prayer asking God to continue to guide group members along their individual and communal journeys.

The Drama of Martha and Mary

At home

- Sit in silence for a few minutes before the group session. Breathe slowly and quietly. Become comfortable with a contemplative pace. Walk through the exercise yourself before the session, visualizing the process.
- Decide on the best way to break the larger group into smaller groups for more intimate conversation and creative writing.

Introducing the exercise

- Draw the group's attention to the story from the gospel of Luke in which Jesus visits Martha and Mary. Before you read the Scripture, ask participants what they know about this story. With whom do they usually identify? Why?
- Break into smaller groups of at least three people to create minidramas.

During the exercise

- Each group is to find a way to retell the Martha-Mary story in their own words for the larger group. Ask them to create a casual, improvisational drama—no more than five minutes long—that retains the *meaning* of the story as the group understands it but updates it for our time. Groups are encouraged to be creative with names, places, and gender roles. (Allow 20 minutes for the breakout groups to create their dramatic pieces.)
- Gather the group back into a semicircle, creating room for the dramas. Ask each breakout group to present its minidrama of the Martha-Mary story.
- Lead the group in a reflection on what they experienced, using the questions listed in the exercise.

After the exercise

- Shift the group's focus from individual reflections to a look at the group as a whole. What is "the better part" for *this group* this day? If you had to describe your church or your spiritual communities' attitude, would it be more like Martha or Mary? Explain. What are some ways our churches or spiritual communities could learn from both Martha and Mary?
- Bring the group to closure with a silent prayer, asking group members to visualize themselves seated at Jesus' feet, listening to him. End the silence by simply saying, "Amen." (5 minutes)

Create Your Own Psalm

At home

- Prior to the gathering, ask participants to bring their Bibles and writing materials.

Introducing the exercise

- Explain that participants will be writing their own psalm in their own words. Ask if anyone has ever done anything like that before.

During the exercise

- Allow plenty of time for each step in the exercise, especially allowing some silence as people think about what their deepest longing or truest feeling before God is at this moment.
- Encourage group members to write from their heart. They don't have to be a poet to enjoy this exercise.

After the exercise

- Lead a time of reflection. Ask if anyone wants to read his or her psalm aloud. (Make sure they know it's not required.) When you get a volunteer, see if the rest of the group can detect what longing or feeling is being expressed to God. When everyone who wants to read their psalm aloud has done so, move on to the reflection questions.
- What was it like to pray in this way? How does writing your own psalm help or hinder your experience of God? What did you learn by reading the biblical psalms? Where did you feel the presence of God most deeply in this prayer? Did anything about your psalm surprise you?
- Close by reading a portion of a psalm of gratitude, either from the Bible or one that was read aloud in the group.

CHAPTER 2. BASIC CONTEMPLATIVE PRACTICES

"Here I Am" Prayer

At home

- Become comfortable with this prayer by practicing it throughout your day for a few days.
- Decide what progression of steps you want to use to lead the group. It doesn't matter where you begin, as long as you spend time in God's presence.
- Decide how long you want the practice to take.

Introducing the exercise

- You may want to share with participants some of the information about Anthony Bloom that's found in the exercise introduction.

During the exercise

- You will lead participants from one step to the next. Take your time and allow for plenty of silence.

After the exercise

- Lead a short reflection on the practice. Which step seemed to be easiest for you? In which step were you best able to relax and let go? What was being in God's presence like for you? How often do you stop and take stock of your own presence, your environment's presence, and God's presence?
- Close your time together with a short prayer of gratitude.

Centering Prayer

At home

- Announce ahead of time that you are going to explore silent, wordless prayer. Because this prayer is so counter to our

Western Christian culture of using words and images to communicate with God, it is best if people are mentally prepared to experience twenty minutes or more of silence.

Introducing the exercise

- Have participants arrange their chairs in a circle.
- Ask how many people either have practiced some form of meditation or know someone who does. Explain that *centering prayer* is a traditional Christian prayer that is almost identical to meditation. The difference is that we begin centering prayer with the clearly stated intention of being in God's presence.
- It may be helpful to say a few words prior to the prayer about letting go of our desire for specific results or outcomes from this (or any) prayer. Place the outcome in God's hands and be open to this prayer changing you and the world in untold ways. Part of enjoying this prayer is embracing the mystery of it.
- Assure the group that you will lead them through it. You will tell them how long the silence will be and will keep the time for them. All they need to do is relax, remain open, and do their best to follow the instructions you give.

During the exercise

- Instruct participants to choose a word that fits their image of God, Christ, or the Holy Spirit. Any word will do. *Stress that they needn't worry about picking the best word—just choose something that is meaningful.* This will be their sacred word for the next few minutes.
- Tell the group how much time they will be spending in silence. You may want to spend the entire time uninterrupted, or, if the group seems unfamiliar with silence, you may break it up into three segments in which you tell them how much time is left and remind them simply to keep returning to their sacred word.
- Ring a soft bell or say "Amen" to end the time of silence. Allow participants some time to gently return their attention to the group.

After the exercise

- Lead a reflection on this prayer practice, using the questions listed in the exercise.
- Be prepared for a range of reactions to this prayer. Typically, some people in a group will love centering prayer, and others will claim they are no good at it or just don't get it. Encourage people to give the prayer practice more than one chance. Emphasize that this is more of a practice than an exercise, and that means you may need to keep practicing it in order to benefit more from it. Also, unlike a physical exercise, this prayer does not require exertion!
- In the discussion, allow equal time to those who find it freeing and those who may find it frustrating. Centering prayer is gaining in popularity nationwide, so you may end up with a group that is not only familiar with it but desirous of a lot more.
- Shift the group's focus from individual reflections to a look at the group as a whole. What was it like to sit in a group and be in silent prayer like this? This is such a simple prayer to do alone at home; why do you think centering prayer groups are popular? In our word-oriented culture (especially in church), what benefit might centering prayer offer? In what way might a shift from word prayer to wordless prayer shift our relationship with God?
- Close with a benediction or a simple "Amen."

Deep Listening

At home

- Practice deep listening with a family member or friend so you have some experience with it.

Introducing the exercise

- Reinforce for the group the importance of the guideline: When the time comes for one person to share, the other person will listen and pray silently for the other person's story. No interrupting, interjecting, or gesturing is appropriate. The listener remains silent and fixed on the speaker's story at all times.

- Share with the group what you learned from your own personal experience with deep listening.
- Break the group into dyads (pairs). If the group has an odd number, you will need to participate in a dyad.

During the exercise

- Provided you were not part of a dyad, notice whether or not the dyads are following the guideline.

After the exercise

- Lead a discussion about the experience of deep listening, using the questions listed in the exercise.
- If you noticed some of the dyads not following the "no inter-jecting" guideline, gently mention that, and have the group talk about the difficulty of simply listening.
- Consider, as a group, how deep listening might be used in group situations (three or more people gathered).
- Close with a prayer of gratitude for good listeners.

Prayer of the Heart

At home

- Decide how long you want this exercise to last. The time spent praying the phrases along with the silence that follows could run as long as 20 minutes.

Introducing the exercise

- You may want to explain the process of choosing a "prayer of the heart" prior to beginning.
- Inform the group of the length of silence and tell them you will be keeping the time. Give them a verbal cue to move into and out of the silence.

- It may help for you to offer participants a few prayers of the heart that others have come up with, such as:

  Come, Lord Jesus

  Freedom, in Christ

  God in your grace, grant us peace

During the exercise

- Ask participants to pray their phrase silently.
- One variation is to allow group members to move about the room or find a quiet place nearby for the prayer. You then could use a chime to signal transitions and the end of the silence.

After the exercise

- Bring the group together to reflect on this prayer. What name for God did they choose, and why? What desire did they express? What was it like to repeat a phrase over and over in prayer? What was the quality of their silent time with God after the breath prayer? In what way might they use this prayer again?
- Close by inviting each person who desires to say their prayer of the heart out loud.

The Jesus Prayer

At home

- Decide how long you want the prayer to last and how you will gather the group when the silence has ended.

Introducing the exercise

- Using the introduction provided, give a little history of the Jesus Prayer.
- Acknowledge that this prayer may be foreign to some people. Reassure the group that participating in this prayer links them spiritually with Christians around the world and throughout history.

During the exercise

- Allow group members to choose any place they want to settle, as space permits. They may also walk around.
- Explain how long the exercise will last and what time the participants need to be back in the group.

After the exercise

- Lead a reflection based on the questions listed in the exercise.
- Close with a spoken prayer.

Praying with Icons

At home

- If your budget permits, produce full-color copies of the image for each group member. Or you may bring in larger icons and have a small group gather around it for prayer. Either way, just make sure everyone has room to gaze. Don't worry that the photocopy is not as clear as the original. Remember, the image is merely the window to the Holy.

Introducing the exercise

- If your group has not prayed with icons before, it would be helpful to share some of the historical information about the prayer from the introduction before beginning the contemplative exercise.

During the exercise

- You are the timekeeper. Make sure you allow plenty of time for gazing.

After the exercise

- Lead the group reflection on the questions listed in the exercise.
- Ask the group what it was like to pray with an icon *with others?* How might a prayer such as this contribute to the life of a community of believers?
- Close with a short spoken prayer.

Contemplative Work Process

At home

- If you are trying this out as a group prayer experience, determine what the work task will be. It could be reflecting on a question about the future of the group or deciding how the group might become more involved in the community.
- If you are using this process to lead a working group, such as a church board or committee in a business meeting, make sure the agenda allows time for the whole process. As boards continue to use this process, they find that the process helps them prioritize time for prayer.
- Decide time limits for each segment. Check-in, for example, can be limited to about two minutes per person if the group is large.
- Decide which prayer exercise you will use for the prayer step.

Introducing the exercise

- Outline the process before you begin it. For many people, this will be an entirely new way of working. Ask participants to remain open to the process of infusing work with prayer.

During the exercise

- You are the facilitator and timekeeper. It is also your responsibility to remind participants of the deep-listening rule of one speaker at a time with no commenting or interrupting.
- It may be helpful during the work part of the meeting to call people's attention to the invitation or the call from God that they identified earlier in the meeting.

After the exercise

- If time permits, have the group reflect on the process before the closing prayer. What was the high point? What was the low point? How did it feel to reflect *as a group* on the communal call from God?
- Thank the group for participating in the process. Close with prayer.

CHAPTER 3. LECTIO DIVINAS

Lectio Divina

At home

- Select a scripture passage that is relatively short. For starters, you might want to select one of these famous prayers of the New Testament:

    Matthew 6:9-13 (The Lord's Prayer)
    Matthew 26:36-42 (Gethsemane)
    Mark 14:32-42 (Gethsemane)
    Luke 11:1-4 (The Lord's Prayer)
    Luke 23:44-46 (Jesus' last prayer)
    John 17:25-26 (or other short segments
       of this long prayer)
    Acts 4:23-31 (Believers pray for boldness)
    Acts 7:54-60 (Stephen's prayer at his stoning)

Introducing the exercise

- When the group gathers, begin by saying a few words about the tradition of *lectio divina,* using the introductory material in this chapter. Briefly outline the steps so participants will have a general idea of where the prayer is headed. Tell them you will keep the time and will move them through each step and any participation that is called for.
- Explain that a passage will be read and that participants are to listen for a word, phrase, or image that seems to speak to them. It could be something that attracts them, stirs them up, or feels like an invitation.
- Explain that at certain places in the prayer, you will ask them to speak aloud their word, phrase, or image or share a reflection.

During the exercise

- Step One is a time of silence. You will keep the time. (2-4 minutes)

- Step Two is a time of reading. You will either read aloud the passage or assign it to someone in the group. Whoever reads should do so slowly. Read twice, with a long silent pause in between. At the end of the first reading, remind the group to listen silently for a word, phrase, or image that calls out to them. After the second reading, allow silence. (2 minutes)
- Move participants into Step Three, reminding them to repeat their word over to themselves silently for a little while longer (2 minutes). Then, ask participants to share their word, phrase, or image with the group—with no elaboration. Just name the word, phrase, or image aloud.
- Move the group into Step Four by inviting them to allow their whole beings to become silent prayer. What is the word, phrase, or image saying to them and their life right now? What is God saying to them in that word, phrase or image? Ask them to keep silence for a short time (2-4 minutes). Then, ask participants to share what they think their word, phrase, or image is revealing to them about their life. (Make sure they understand that they do not *have* to say very much or anything at all if they don't want to.) During this sharing time, there is no commenting, interrupting, or reflecting on someone else's sharing. Let this step take longer, with pauses in between each individual's sharing.
- When everyone who wants to share has done so, move the group into Step Five by inviting participants to let go of all words, thoughts, and reflections and simply be absorbed by the presence and embrace of God's love. (2-4 minutes)

After the exercise

- Reflect as a group on how it felt to pray with Scripture in this way. What did participants notice about the silence? What did they notice about the sharing of the word? Which step did they feel most at home with? Which step was more difficult for them?
- Would they do this prayer exercise again? Why or why not?
- How is this approach to Scripture different from Bible study?

- Close with a circle in which everyone again states the word, phrase, or image that was meaningful to them in the exercise.

Lectio Divina on Community

At home

- Decide how this practice will be used. This is an excellent prayer to use with a group that needs to take a close look at a specific event in the life of the group. In that case, you as leader might preselect an event—such as the last gathering, a business meeting, a worship service—for the group to reflect on.
- Another approach is to have each individual in the group do the exercise on a community event that they have chosen. If you do this, allow some time before beginning for people to select an experience. If they seem stymied by the task, you might give them some ideas, such as a worship service, a family gathering, a workplace encounter, a meeting, or a recent situation involving a friend.

Introducing the exercise

- Remind participants that this is like *lectio divina* with Scripture, except that the prayer information to be "read" is their life in community.

During the exercise

- Lead participants through each step, allowing plenty of silence for the reflections. Encourage them to write in their journals if they so desire.
- This *lectio divina* is done in silence throughout, with discussion at the end.

After the exercise

- If you are leading a group in a reflection on an event you pre-selected, then ask each participant to share (as they feel comfortable) the portion of the selected event that had energy for them. After everyone has shared their "word" from the reflection, ask them to talk about what that word (portion of the experience) seemed to be saying to them personally. Then ask them what they think their word may be saying to the group as a whole.

- If you are leading a group in which each person selected their own community experience, then following the time of contemplation at the end, invite the group to reflect aloud on what they experienced in the prayer time. What did their word (portion of the experience) have to offer their life today? How was God present to them in the prayer?
- Close with a prayer of gratitude for the ways God is present with us in community.

Luther's Four-stranded Garland

At home

- Decide which Scripture to use.
- Alert group members that they may want to bring their journals for this exercise.

Introducing the exercise

- Set the stage by using the introductory material about Martin Luther's background. Also, if time permits, explain the steps of the exercise and ask people to comment on how this is similar to and different from traditional *lectio divina*.

During the exercise

- Lead the group through the steps, allowing pauses for silence during each step. Give at least four minutes for each of the four garland steps.
- Invite people to write their responses in a journal or on paper that is provided.

After the exercise

- Lead a reflection on how the prayer exercise felt for group members. Did one step seem easier than others? Where did they feel the presence of God in the prayer?
- Invite participants to share from their journal. Since this exercise involves a step of confession, you may want to remind the group to share only that which they feel safe and comfortable sharing.
- End with a final prayer.

Lectio Divina with Music

At home

- Choose an appropriate piece of music, ideally an instrumental piece. Make sure it isn't too long (7 minutes or shorter) since you will play it twice.

Introducing the exercise

- Acknowledge that this exercise will be easier for some people than for others. Ask participants to remain open to the idea of doing *lectio divina* without words.

During the exercise

- Lead the group through the steps listed in the exercise, allowing plenty of time for each step (about 4 minutes per step). Invite them to write in a journal about their prayer if they like.
- Rather than asking the group to speak about their word, phrase, image, emotion, or memory between steps (as we did with traditional *lectio divina*), hold that question for a reflection time at the end.

After the exercise

- Lead a reflection time on the prayer. What was it like to pray with music? Did the music evoke anything in particular in you? What was your "word" or the gift in prayer that you repeatedly returned to? How did it connect with your life? Where was God's presence most strongly felt in this prayer?

- Close with a prayer of gratitude, thanking God for the gift of music in our lives.

Lectio Divina in Nature

At home

- Decide where this prayer will be done. It doesn't have to involve an elaborate road trip to a park (although that might be fun). It could be a courtyard of a church or someone's backyard garden. Make arrangements for the group to gather at the location or be transported.
- Photocopy the steps for each participant, since they will be going off on their own for about twenty minutes.
- Encourage them to bring journals if they want.

Introducing the exercise

- When you are at the site with the group, explain the steps of the prayer and tell them when they are to regather as a group.

During the exercise

- Certainly experience the prayer yourself, but stay close at hand to answer any questions.
- Keep an eye on the time. Be at the gathering site before the group arrives.

After the exercise

- Lead a time of reflection. How did it feel it to pray in nature? What drew your attention? What connections with your own life did you make? Where did you feel the presence of God most vividly? Which step held the most meaning for you? Which step felt the most difficult?
- Close with a prayer of gratitude.

CHAPTER 4. LIFE REFLECTIONS

The Traditional Ignatian Examen

At home

- Spend a few days doing this examen yourself.
- Decide how much time you will allow the group to reflect on each step of the prayer.
- Decide if you want the group to share aloud their findings after each step or if you want to hold all group reflection until the end.
- Invite participants to bring their journals in case they want to write about this prayer.

Introducing the exercise

- Be prepared to give a few basics about Ignatius of Loyola (1491–1556):

  1. He was a Spaniard, former soldier, injured at the Battle of Pamplona in 1521.
  2. His conversion occurred in 1521, the same year Martin Luther was excommunicated and the Reformation began. Ignatius is considered part of the Catholic "counter-reformation," an important reform movement within the Catholic Church.
  3. He founded the Society of Jesus (Jesuit) religious order.
  4. Ignatius had a strong interest in being guided by God, and wrote about how we can know when we are being guided by God.
  5. He used this imaginative exercise in his *Spiritual Exercises* to take retreatants (people taking an individual retreat with a Jesuit spiritual director) through the life of Jesus.
  6. He was canonized by the Catholic Church in 1622.

During the exercise

- Move the group from step to step. Suggest that they write their impressions or discoveries from this prayer in their journal, if they so desire.
- Lead the discussion, if there is to be discussion in the midst of the steps.

After the exercise

- Lead a time of reflection. If you already held reflection between each step, then ask the group how it was for them to pray in this way. Where did they feel the Spirit move most deeply within them in this prayer? Where did they feel the Spirit may have been blocked?
- Ask: How might a group or committee use this prayer in a communal fashion?

A Contemporary Examen

At home

- Keep your own examen journal so you can share with the group how the prayer has helped you "find God in all things."
- Decide how you want to use this exercise. You may choose to have individuals do their own examens and then, at the end, share with the group their "highs and lows" (or whatever wording of the questions you suggest). If you are leading a group that functions as a governing or working body, the group may want to do an examen on a period of time in the life of their organization.

Introducing the exercise

- If possible, obtain a copy of *Sleeping with Bread*, the book from which this contemporary examen comes. Share the introductory story about the loaves of bread used to comfort children during World War II.

- If your group has not already done an Ignatian practice in which you introduced facts about Ignatius of Loyola, give some background using the information found in the exercise directly preceding this one.

During the exercise

- If you are leading individuals in a group setting, you may choose either to have them share on each question after an appropriate time of silent reflection or have them share on both questions in a reflection time at the end. Both ways work well, but the second way allows for more silence.
- If you are leading a group that wants to reflect on a discrete period of time in the life of the group (for example, a capital campaign, the last gathering, an event it sponsored, or a review of the last quarter), then you will need to adjust the questions in a way that reminds them of the period of time they are praying about. An example would be a church board that wants to reflect on a stewardship campaign that just ended. You might ask:

   What aspect of the campaign most enlivened our board (or church)?

   What aspect of the campaign most drained our board (or church)?

After the exercise

- Lead a time of reflection on the "highs and lows" (or however you worded the question) that participants named in their prayers.
- If you are leading a group reflection on a time in the life of the group, ask what all this means for the life and future of the group. How will the group use this prayerfully gathered information?
- If you are leading individuals who reflected on their day or life, ask them how they will use this prayerfully gathered information in their daily lives.

- Ask participants how it was to pray in this manner and to share what they discovered in prayer.
- Close with a prayer of gratitude for the many ways God is experienced in our lives.

Prayer of Remembrance

At home

- There are two ways to approach this with groups. Decide which one is best for your group.

    Lead a group in which individuals come up with their own memories and then discuss what they discovered in prayer at the end (after the colloquy).

    Lead a group that wants to reflect upon an event in the life of the group or community. For example, a board of deacons might want to reflect on an emotional healing service it held. Or a youth group might need to be in prayer about the death of a member.

Introducing the exercise

- Explain to the group that you will be leading this much like a guided meditation or reflection.

During the exercise

- Keep the time and gently move the group through the stages of the prayer. Save reflection on the prayer for the end.

After the exercise

- Draw the group together for reflection.
- Ask the group: Which phase of this prayer was most meaningful? Which phase was most difficult? What would you like to share about your discoveries in this prayer? What did you choose to remember (if there was no common memory being used in prayer)? How did you feel God's presence in this prayer? In what way did you feel God's guidance or direction? What happened in the colloquy?

- If it was a group reflection, draw attention to threads and connections you noticed in the sharing. What is the Spirit doing in this prayer for this group? Is there some group learning that needs to be acknowledged?
- Close with a short word prayer or a time of silence ended with "Amen."

Praying Ultimate Questions

At home

- Decide which question you will use.
- Decide how the group will be configured for the discussion time. If your group is quite large, you may want to form breakout groups of three or four people per group. This could create a noise problem, so you may want to have breakout rooms available.
- Invite participants to bring writing materials or a journal.

Introducing the exercise

- You may want to spend a few moments explaining that the group will be praying with or reflecting upon a serious question. Ask participants how they feel about a faith that encourages questions. What are they more comfortable with: questions or answers?

During the exercise

- Offer the question for reflection.
- Allow twenty minutes of silence for individuals to pray with the question. They may want to spread out in the room and make themselves comfortable. Some may choose to take a walk. Be sure to tell them what time the group is reconvening.
- At the end of the silence, draw the group together. Explain that you are moving into another twenty minutes of sharing time, but that this continues to be a prayerful time, not a time for debate or overly animated discussion. Ask that everyone observe the following guidelines:

Speak *only* for yourself, using "I" statements and refraining from any comment on what another person has shared. This means no advice, no fixing, no saving, and no "setting one another straight." This also means no theological debate. Everyone is speaking for themselves, and we are leaving what is said in God's hands.

Allow for silence and pauses between speakers. (As leader you may need to ask for some times of silence.)

- If you are remaining in one large group, proceed to the prayerful sharing time. If you are breaking into small groups, this is the time to do that.

After the exercise

- After twenty minutes of sharing, shift the discussion from individuals sharing to large-group sharing. (If you are using breakout groups, bring them together for this closing portion of the reflection.)
- Ask the large group what it noticed about the nature of sharing with one another on the topic of ultimate questions. In what way was God present in the question? In the reflection? In the sharing?
- What is it like to listen to other people's sharing on important questions without commenting or engaging in conversation? What happens when people share from their hearts without fear of being corrected or redirected in conversation? What is it like to pray in this way?
- Close with a short word prayer. If your group is going to take on more questions in this fashion, you might consider giving them the question for the next gathering at this time.

The Prayer Journal

At home

- Give participants the step-by-step method for journal-keeping ahead of time so they can begin before they come to the group.
- Arrange to have tables for the group to use in this exercise.

Introducing the exercise

- Acknowledge that many people see writing in a journal as a solitary enterprise, but that in this gathering the group will write in a journal together.
- Using the introduction to the exercise, share some of the history of writing in a journal in the Protestant tradition.

During the exercise

- Begin with silent prayer.
- Ask participants to write in a journal on the step that reads: "To explore spiritual growth based on events in your life." Read the questions aloud. Ask participants to journal in silence.
- Allow at least twenty minutes for the journaling.

After the exercise

- Draw the group into a circle. Ask them to bring their journals.
- If participants would like to read short sections of their journal entries to the group, allow them to do so. Or they may want to share the essence of what they wrote in their own words, without reading sections. Stress that no one has to share anything from their writing unless they want to. Before people share from their journals, ask that there be no commenting by others on what is shared by the writers.
- Lead a time of reflection on the journal activity. What was it like to pray in this way? How did the act of writing the prayer help or hinder your praying? In what way did you feel God's presence in the writing?
- Ask participants who have been writing in a journal for awhile what they notice about patterns and themes that emerge in their journals. How have you noticed God's action in your life through reviewing your journal notations?
- In closing, ask the group to keep confidential what they have heard from one another's journals.

Art as Prayer

At home

- Decide if this exercise will be used primarily for individuals exploring their own questions or for a working group pursuing a common intention. For example, a committee that experienced a conflict at the last gathering may want to use this prayer to explore ways in which God was particularly active at the last gathering. When praying in this communal way, spend plenty of time with the reflection questions at the end, with a particular emphasis on a theme or thread that came up within the group.
- Gather the supplies you'll need, or ask the participants to bring the supplies.
- Make sure there are tables available for this exercise.

Introducing the exercise

- Impress upon participants that they do not need to be artists to pray in this way. Ask them to give their "inner critic" this time off.

During the exercise

- Allow plenty of silence and space for participants to settle in and determine their intention for the exercise. Explain that their intention can be anything they hope to learn more about in prayer. Frequently it is based on exploring a feeling about something they are longing to understand more clearly.
- Be on hand to encourage anyone who looks as if they need some help. Although the experience is done mostly in silence, an encouraging word from you would not be out of line.

After the exercise

- When participants have finished creating the visual representation of the inner image, draw the group into reflection.
- Ask them the questions listed in the exercise for reflection.
- Was there any common thread or theme that ran through the group's images? For groups using a common intention: What might God be saying to this group in this prayer?

CHAPTER 5. DISCERNMENT PROCESSES

Ignatian Spiritual Discernment

At home

- Determine if this is to be for individuals in discernment or for a group in communal discernment.

    If you are leading individuals in discernment, ask participants to come to the first meeting of the group with a question, preferably a question about a concrete life situation that can be answered with a yes or no. If you are leading a long retreat, you could do this process over a few days. If not, break it down into segments over time.

    If you are leading a group in communal discernment, determine if the group already has a clear question. If so, proceed with the exercise, breaking it down into segments over time. If not, you will need to spend a fair amount of time helping the group hone the question. Groups generally have a harder time agreeing on one clear-cut question than individuals do, so be patient.

- Set up a schedule for the process that gives everyone time to think and pray his or her way through. This could take time. However, if you spread out the process too long (say, over a year or more) people could become frustrated with the pace. Decide what will work best for the group you are leading.

Introducing the exercise

- Give some background information on Ignatius of Loyola. (See "Introducing the exercise" for the Traditional Ignatian Examen, found in the chapter 4 section of this leader's guide.)
- Explain that this process is *not* literally contained in the classic *Spiritual Exercises* by Ignatius; rather, it is a process based on principles of discernment found throughout the *Exercises*.

During the exercise

- Lead the individuals or the group through the questions.
- Begin each session by returning to the first two steps: *Prepare,* and *Desire to follow God's leading and indifference to all else.* This is a critical element of Ignatian discernment and a way to reinforce the notion that the entire discernment process is surrounded by prayer.

After the exercise

- After finishing each segment, reflect on the process. How does it feel to take this approach to faithful decision-making? What is hardest for you? What is easiest for you? Where have you felt God's leading most actively? How is this similar to any other way you have approached decision making? How is it different? What insights came to you in this segment?
- After finishing the entire process, including *testing the decision,* spend time reflecting on the process. Which part of it inspired you most? Which part was most taxing? Where did you feel God's presence most intimately? Would you use a process like this again? What do you understand *consolation* to mean in your life? What do you understand *desolation* to mean in your life? How will you use these measures to help you discern in the future?

Quaker Clearness Committee

At home

- Decide what you are doing—discernment with individuals or discernment for a group.

  If an individual in the group has a question they would like to bring before a clearness committee, then follow the process outlined in chapter 5.

  If an issue within your group has come to the forefront and the group wants a process for discerning, then follow the process listed below under the title "The Clearness Committee Exercise for Group Consideration of a Question."

Introducing the exercise

- Present some background information about the Quaker tradition:
  1. Founded by George Fox in the mid-seventeenth century. Also known as the Society of Friends.
  2. Emphasis on direct experience of God's spirit.
  3. Belief in a divine inner light that gives us guidance, provided we are still and calm enough to receive it. Emphasis on silence in worship.
  4. No set liturgy. No creeds. No celebration of outward sacraments.
  5. Clearness Committees were originally designed to help young Friends decide on marriage.
- Give a description of how Clearness Committee will proceed.

During the exercise

- With either the process listed below or the one in chapter 10, you are the clerk. Most important, you will gently enforce the guidelines.
- As the clerk, you will keep an eye on the time and move the process along its steps.

After the exercise

- If you are doing discernment with an individual, the only reflection time necessary is built into the chapter 5 process.
- If you are doing discernment as a group, you will lead a time of reflection at the end as listed in the process below.

The Clearness Committee Exercise for Group Consideration of a Question (2 hours)

- The question or issue to be discerned should be decided ahead of time. It should be an issue facing the whole group (for example, "Is God calling us to reach out at this time with a soup kitchen based in our fellowship hall?").

- When it's time for the meeting to begin, you, the clerk, will read the question aloud and then go over the following guidelines for discerners in a group setting:

    1. Silence is an important part of the process. It allows everyone the space to listen to God. Discerners need to commit to a pace that is relaxed and spacious.

    2. Discerners are only to ask simple, honest, and caring questions. A question should not include statements, prefaced remarks, or stories. A question should never consist of advice or judgment cloaked in the form of a question. If any of these guidelines is not observed, the clerk will gently intercede and ask that the question be reframed. Once a question has been asked of the group, the clerk will allow time for answers to emerge from within the group before moving on to another question. This will take some time.

    3. Discerners should not in any way try to "fix" the situation, give advice, or "set anyone straight" about anything. There is no place in this process for commentary on what others have said.

    4. Discerners should take care that their questions are prompted by their prayer insights or the urging of the Spirit and not simply out of curiosity.

- After reviewing the guidelines, the clerk moves the group into a time of silent prayer (at least 7 minutes) for all involved to become aware of the presence of God and be at peace with that presence so that the group is ready to listen to God as members listen to one another.

- The clerk opens the floor for questions, saying, "What questions do we have about this issue under discernment?" Allow time for careful consideration of the questions.

- At the end of one hour, the clerk will call for a silent stretching break of 5 minutes.

- After the break, the clerk will allow a time of silence before saying, "What questions are we feeling deep within our hearts about this issue under discernment?" Allow time for reflective responses to these questions.

- After one hour and forty minutes in the process, the clerk will call for silence as the group considers whether consensus—a leading of the Spirit in one direction—has emerged. Each discerner is given time to answer yes or no and say a few brief words about where he or she thinks God is leading the group. If consensus is reached, spend the last few moments reflecting on what just happened. If no consensus is reached, reflect on what piece of the issue under discernment needs more prayer and perhaps another Clearness Committee process.
- If time permits, lead a discussion on how it felt to discern together as a group. Where did you feel God's presence most deeply? What part of the clearness committee seemed most helpful to you? to the group? What part was most difficult for you? For the group?
- The clerk ends the session with prayer and, if needed, sets up another time to meet.

The Wesleyan Quadrilateral

At home

- Determine how the group will do this exercise, either as individuals or as a group. Whether done as individuals or a group, a discernment question should be determined before starting the process.

Introducing the exercise

- You may want to draw a large diagram of the quadrilateral for this exercise.
- Have some resources on hand, such as a Bible commentary and concordance.

During the exercise

- If you are leading individuals in this exercise, take them through the steps, allowing adequate time to consider each point of the quadrilateral.

- If you are leading a group in a communal discernment, take them through the steps, allowing times of silence for reflection and prayer and times for comments on each point of the quadrilateral.

After the exercise

- Lead a time of reflection with participants. How was it to pray through a discernment issue using this four-point method? Which point did they gravitate to most naturally? Which one was most difficult? Why? Does the quadrilateral cover enough areas of discernment to suit you? Did you come to any resolution on your question as a result of using this method?
- Close with a prayer of gratitude for the many ways God guides us in discernment.

CHAPTER 6. BODY PRAYERS

Breath Prayer

At home

- Decide if you want to use this prayer alone for the full 20 minutes or in a shorter form as a gathering activity.

Introducing the exercise

- Explain to participants how the simple prayer works. Also explain that distractions are normal and that all they need to do is return their attention to their breath when a distraction comes up.

During the exercise

- You are the timekeeper.
- Bring the group out of the time of silence gently, as some people will be deeper into the experience than others.

After the exercise

- If time permits, lead a reflection on the prayer. How was it to pray in this wordless, imageless way? Did this prayer draw you closer to God? Was this style of praying helpful to you? Why or why not?
- Close with a prayer of gratitude to God for the breath of life.

Focusing Prayer

At home

- If you think you need more background on biospirituality, consult the Web site www.biospiritual.org for information.

Introducing the exercise

- Explain that in this exercise the group will be listening to "felt senses" in the body during prayer. Acknowledge that this prayer comes from a rather new and exciting branch of Christian spirituality called biospirituality, which means experiencing God in and through our bodies.
- You may need to share with group members your own experience with focusing prayer in order to help them enter the exercise.

During the exercise

- Open with a prayer that puts God clearly at the center of this exercise.
- You will be leading the group through the focusing prayer one step at a time. Allow plenty of time for each step. The group will keep silence while in the prayer.

After the exercise

- After the last step of the focusing prayer, lead a reflection time. What was it like to pray in this way? Where was God in the experience of your "felt sense"? What wisdom did your body have to impart to you? How is it that you have experienced God's guidance in your body before now? What part of this prayer was most helpful for you? Least helpful? Would you do it again?
- Close with a prayer thanking God for giving us wise and wonderful bodies.

Praying with Beads

At home

- Decide how participants in your group will obtain beads. You could ask them to come with rosaries, beaded prayer rings, a string of beads they made, or any smooth beaded necklace. Alternatively, participants could spend part of the group time making a simple string of beads. For information on how to make prayer beads, see the article "A String and a Prayer" by Eleanor Wiley and Maggie Oman in *Spirituality & Health* magazine (fall 2002), found online at www.spiritualityhealth.com.

- Ask participants to bring their Bibles to the group.

Introducing the exercise

- Prior to starting the prayer, lead a discussion about what participants know about praying with beads. Have you ever done it before? What was the prayer like?

During the exercise

- Lead participants through each step, allowing plenty of silence between prayers. The word prayers may be said aloud in unison.

After the exercise

- Lead a time of reflection on the prayer. How did it feel to pray with beads? Were you able to enter the prayer fully? What part of the prayer connected you most deeply with God? What part of the prayer distracted you from God?
- Close by saying or singing the doxology.

Prayer Walk

At home

- Decide where the group will do this walk and for how long.
- Select a meeting place and time for discussion at the end of the walk.
- Instruct participants to come in comfortable clothes and shoes. If inclement weather is a possibility, select an alternate site indoors where there is room to walk.

Introducing the exercise

- Describe the steps of the prayer before setting out on the walk. You may want to photocopy the steps for participants to keep on hand.

During the exercise

- You are the timekeeper. Make sure everyone knows what time to return for the group reflection. You may want to sound a chime when it's time to gather.

After the exercise

- Lead a reflection time on the questions listed in the last step of the exercise.
- Close with a circle prayer in which participants say aloud what they were most grateful for on their walk.

Praying the Labyrinth

At home

- Decide what kind of labyrinth is right for your group. Ideally, you will find a large permanent labyrinth at a site near you and have the group gather there. If you can't locate one, you may be able to find a cloth labyrinth to place on the floor in a large space. If neither is available to you, make copies of a finger labyrinth (see Tips) and have participants do the prayer as a finger "walk." If any members of your group are not able to walk, make sure they have a finger labyrinth to use while others walk.
- Advise participants when and where they are to meet.

Introducing the exercise

- When everyone has arrived, gather at the opening of the labyrinth, where you will explain the steps of the prayer. (You may want to give them copies explaining the three steps of the "mystical path"—purgation, illumination, and union.)
- Explain that this prayer is usually done rather slowly, but everyone has their own pace. It is all right to pass someone by going around them.

During the exercise

- Invite participants to enter the labyrinth at their own pace. It is best to allow space between walkers.
- Allow enough time for everyone to finish.

After the exercise

- Lead a time of reflection on the questions listed at the end of the exercise.
- Close with a prayer of gratitude for all the ways God walks with us along our daily paths.

Embodying Scripture

At home

- Make sure you are familiar with the passage chosen. If you are using the Naomi and Ruth passage, you may read aloud the phrases for movement. If you choose a different passage, think about which parts of the passage you want to isolate for the prayer motions.
- Inform participants that there will be some easy, gentle movement, and so they should wear comfortable, loose-fitting clothes.

Introducing the exercise

- Since this type of prayer may be new to people, spend a few minutes before the prayer explaining what you will be doing and how they will be participating. Explain that their movements or stances need not be elaborate or artistic in any way. They should listen to their bodies and not worry about what they look like in that posture of prayer. Their pose may shift or change during the silence—it's okay to be comfortable!

During the exercise

- You will read the long passage to them aloud slowly, and then read the shorter passage in its entirety. After that you will lead them through the phrases for movement.

- You are the keeper of the time and you set the pace. Allow for significant silence (at least 5 minutes) for each phrase and posture.

After the exercise

- Following the final prayer pose of their choosing (and some silence for closure to the exercise), lead the group in a time of reflection, using the questions listed at the end of the exercise.
- If this was new for the group, thank them for their openness to new forms of prayer.
- Close the group experience by asking them to choose a prayer posture again —perhaps one that came from the passage—to hold in silence for a few moments.

Confession Body Prayer

At home

- This is a short prayer, so you need to decide how to use it with a group. It may work best in the context of a meeting or at the beginning or end of a group session.

Introducing the exercise

- Demonstrate the motions, and describe the prayer before asking the group to do it.

During the exercise

- Lead the group through the four steps, allowing some silence between steps.
- You may want to do the prayer several times. It could even be done to music.
- You may also do this in silence—provided everyone is clear on each step. The group does *not* have to do this prayer in unison.

After the exercise

- If you want, you could lead a time of reflection. Sometimes people want to give voice to their confessions and sometimes they do not. Honor everyone's choice. Ask them how it was to confess in this way. Does embodying the confession help make it more real? Where did you experience God's presence in this prayer?

CHAPTER 7. PRAYERS OF THE IMAGINATION

Ignatian Imagination Prayer

At home

- Advise participants that they may want to write for part of this exercise, so they should bring writing materials if that's the case.

Introducing the exercise

- Give some background information on Ignatius of Loyola. (See "Introducing the exercise" for the Traditional Ignatian Examen, found in chapter 4 of this leader's guide.)

During the exercise

- You will walk the participants through the imagination exercise, much like a guided meditation. It is important that you pause and allow a time of silence after each question or guiding step to allow imaginations to flow.

After the exercise

- If you have allowed time after the concluding Lord's Prayer, lead a time of group reflection on this prayer. How was it to pray with your imagination? What was the easiest part of the prayer to enter? What part was most difficult? What role did you play in the scene—observer, participant, one of the characters? Who did you hold a dialogue with? What surprised you? What moved you? What disturbed you?

Wall of Prayer

At home

- Decide whether you are using this exercise primarily for individuals in the group, or if it is to be tailored for the group as a whole. For example, a spirituality circle might want to do the exercise exactly as outlined in the chapter; whereas the governing board of a church or organization might want to tailor the exercise to a situation at hand.

- Collect the paper and art utensils to be used in the creation of this wall of prayer. If you have a large group, make sure you have a large amount of paper. You may also divide the large group into breakout groups to work on posters or separate walls of prayer.

- Inform participants that this prayer will involve some artwork and to dress accordingly.

Introducing the exercise

- Write the question to be used in the prayer at the top of the paper or poster board. If you are using this exercise with a group that makes decisions and has responsibilities (such as a board, session, or committee) consider adapting the question to reflect some issue the group is coping with. For example, if a budget committee is struggling with a stewardship campaign, the question might become: *When we listen to our deepest and truest selves, what longings and desires for this stewardship campaign do we bring to God in prayer?* Make the question open-ended enough to allow the group to ponder the specific situation without leading toward any particular answer.

During the exercise

- Lead participants through the process. Ask them to shift their positions from time to time so they can write or draw on different parts of the paper.

- Give the group a two-minute warning before ending the prayer so they can finish their thought or image.

After the exercise

- Lead the time of reflection. What was it like to pray your deepest desires? What was it like to write or draw it on your "wall"?

- Ask each group to look at its wall. Which desires and prayers are similar? Which are different? Is there a theme that emerges? Did this prayer move from being a prayer of individuals to a group prayer? If so, how? What was the catalyst?
- If you used breakout groups, have the larger group look at the various walls. Is there a theme that emerges within the whole group?
- If this was an exercise for a working group—with an adapted question—ask participants if this prayer helped the group get a better feel for the situation or issue at hand. Did anything on the wall surprise you? Did anything inspire you? Did anything move you? Especially press the group for any theme that emerges.
- Close with a short prayer of gratitude for the desires that God works in and through us.

Desire Prayer

At home

- Decide whether this prayer is for individuals in a group setting or if your group will be praying in and through one stated desire.
- A spirituality or prayer group may choose to have each person pray with his or her own desire in silence.
- A working board, council, or committee may use this prayer to express a specific desire the group has. For example, a board facing an employment-relations conflict may want to pray with the desire that the conflict be resolved.

Introducing this exercise

- At the outset, admit that this prayer may be quite different from prayers participants are used to. Explain that it originated in Native American and Celtic cultures.
- If you are leading a working group in praying with a particular desire, spend a few moments at the beginning deciding how the group would word its desire. Also, change the wording of the instructions to reflect that you are praying the *group's* desire.

- Reflect on Psalm 37:4, "Take delight in the LORD, / and he will give you the desires of your heart." What does that mean for you?

During the exercise

- Lead participants through the prayer. Allow plenty of time in silence (at least 10 minutes) for the imagining of the desire through the five senses.

After the exercise

- Lead the group in a time of reflection. How did it feel to pray their desires? What inspired them? What moved them? What surprised them?
- If you are with a working group that chose one desire to pray with, spend time in reflection on how praying—as a group—felt for them. Did the desire shift in any way? Did anyone receive any insights in prayer that they would like to share? After praying in this way, does the group feel a particular call from God?
- Close with a prayer of gratitude, and ask participants to keep their eyes open in the coming weeks and months for opportunities from God pertaining to their desire.

CHAPTER 8. REFLECTIONS ON MEDIA

Analyzing Pop Culture Texts

At home

- Carefully select the media clip to be used. Make sure it is short (less than 10 minutes). Find one that speaks to the human longing for meaning, understanding, spiritual enlightenment, or God. The clip doesn't have to be about religion, but it should be about meaning or longing.
- Make sure you have all the technological equipment and expertise you need to make the exercise run smoothly. You will need a room that can be darkened for this exercise.
- If you feel the need for a "crash course" in media literacy, go to the Web site of the Center for Media Literacy (www.medialit.org) and download the orientation guide for the CML MediaLit Kit.

Introducing the exercise

- Begin by asking participants how they use media (television, radio, newspapers, film, electronic devices) on a daily basis. How do they feel about their media use?
- Ask participants how they feel about using spiritual practices with media.
- Explain how media will be used in this exercise.

During the exercise

- You will be leading the reflection by posing the various questions listed in the exercise. Pace the discussion by allowing for times of silence.
- Remind participants of the guideline for sharing: "No fixing, saving, advice, or setting one another straight." Ask each person to reflect on the media clip from his or her point of view, using "I" statements rather than commenting on what another has said.

After the exercise

- Lead a time of reflection on the analysis. How was it to use the spiritual discipline of study with media? How was it like prayer? How was it different from other ways you have prayed?
- Close with a short prayer of gratitude.
- If you would like participants to use this analysis method at home, send them away with a handout of the exercise.

Images of God in Media

At home

- Decide which film or television clip you will be using for this exercise. Make sure it is relatively short (no longer than 10 minutes).
- Gather all the equipment needed.

Introducing the exercise

- Ask participants what their favorite image of God is. How often do they see this image portrayed in media?

During the exercise

- You will be leading the reflection by posing the questions listed in the exercise. Keep the pace slow and leisurely.
- Remind participants that they are sharing *their* images of God, and not critiquing or commenting on someone else's image. They may, however, want to share a critique of the media image.

After the exercise

- Spend some time reflecting on the exercise itself. What was it like to analyze a visual portrayal of an image of God? Where did you feel God most active in this exercise? Where did you feel disconnected from God?
- Close with a silent prayer that lets go of images of God.

"God" on Prayer

At home

- Select the film or television clip to be viewed. Make sure it is short.
- Gather the equipment needed for the group's viewing.

Introducing the exercise

- Ask participants to comment on some of the beliefs about prayer that they see portrayed in film and television.

During the exercise

- Watch the clip.
- Lead the reflection by posing the questions to the participants.
- Allow for some silence so the pace remains calm.
- Remind participants to speak from their own experiences rather than critiquing someone else's reflection. There is time, however, for a critique of the media portrayals.

After the exercise

- Lead a group reflection on the exercise. What was it like to compare your own views on prayer with what you saw in the clip? How did other participants' reflections enhance your own? Did the group experience a consensus about the clip?
- Close with a short prayer. If you or someone in the group knows the Taize chant "O Lord Hear My Prayer," end the session singing it.

Meditation on *The Apostle*

At home

- Rent or check out *The Apostle* for yourself and watch it at home. Decide on a few scenes to show the group for reflection. Make sure each scene is relatively short.

- Go through the list of questions and remove any that do not pertain to the scenes you plan to show.
- Or ask everyone in the group to view *The Apostle* in its entirety on their own before attending the group meeting. Ask them to note where in the film they felt spiritually moved or inspired. If you have them watch it before attending, then you may use all the questions listed in the exercise.
- If you wish, do a little research on the making of *The Apostle* so you can provide a more thorough introduction to the film.

Introducing the exercise

- Ask participants to comment on what they know about the making of *The Apostle*. How did film critics receive it? How did the general public?

During the exercise

- Lead the reflection on the film. Pose the questions to the group and allow some silence in between questions.
- Spend ample time on the question about where participants felt particularly moved in the film. What in the scene moved them? What does it remind them of? What, in their own lives, does the scene address?

After the exercise

- Ask the group to try expressing themselves in prayer to God aloud and at the same time—much like a Pentecostal prayer service.
- Reflect on that experience. What is it like to speak out loud to God and to do it in a room full of people who are also speaking out loud to God? Compare that kind of prayer to the silent, contemplative prayer. Which are you more drawn to? Why?
- Close by thanking God for the many ways we can be in prayer and for the diversity of personalities we were created to express.

Meditation on *Entertaining Angels*

At home

- Watch the film and locate the scene to show the group. You may also have the group view the film at home before the group meeting. Showing the whole film to the group before this exercise makes the group meeting long and may tire participants out. Clips are much better for reflection.
- Make sure the room you will be using is suitable for video viewing.

Introducing the exercise

- Begin by giving some background on Dorothy Day.
  1. She was a Catholic laywoman (1897–1980) who became a leader in the Catholic Worker Movement.
  2. She cared for and served indigent and homeless people.
  3. Dorothy Day met some resistance from the institutional Church in her day, but is now seen as a possible candidate for sainthood.

During the exercise

- Lead the prayer, play the clip, and walk the group through the reflection questions.
- Allow for plenty of silence and pauses in the reflection time.

After the exercise

- Before the closing prayer, spend a few moments with the group reflecting on how it feels to pray in this way with a media clip. What other movies are similar to *Entertaining Angels* in that they lend themselves to reflection on living out the Christian life?
- Close with the prayer given in the exercise.

Where Is the Faith?

At home

- Choose a clip from a film or television show that features one character prominently. Make sure the clip is short. Prepare a short commentary on the context of the clip, since you won't have time to show the entire film or television show.
- Or select a film or television show that participants in the group will watch on their own before coming to the gathering.

Introducing the exercise

- Explain that when we speak of faith we are not *necessarily* looking for religious faith or faith in God. That might be the case, but the character may exhibit faith in something very different. For example, in the case of most of the police dramas, the characters place enormous faith in criminal evidence pointing to the truth.

During the exercise

- Lead the prayer, play the clip, and facilitate reflection time by posing the questions. Allow the conversation to unfold with ease, permitting silence between questions.
- Allow ample silence before participants answer the question about what God reveals to them in the viewing of the clip.

After the exercise

- Before the final breath prayer, ask the group to reflect on what it is like to find faith in a media clip. Was it difficult to find? What surprised you? What inspired you? What disturbed you?
- Close with the final prayer that repeats the opening prayer.

You're the Producer

At home

- Obtain blank paper or poster board for this group activity.
- Decide on the makeup of the group or groups. If your group includes ten or more people, break it into smaller groups of two, three, or four. Ideally, you will be creating five groups—so that each group will ponder together a different word. If your group is between five to ten people, create as many dyads (pairs) as possible, with the rest of the people working individually.

Introducing the exercise

- Ask participants to name films or television shows that they believe express the best about Christian ethics and spirituality without explicitly mentioning religion.

During the exercise

- You will lead the opening prayer, explain the exercise, and keep the time. Give the groups or individuals plenty of time to think through how they would depict their concept (up to 30 minutes). They will use the paper or poster board to brainstorm ideas.
- Remind them that if they cannot come up with ways to depict their concept, then they might think about films or television shows that did illustrate the concept without religious language or images.

After the exercise

- Lead a time of reflection in which each group or individual talks about what they came up with.
- Pose the questions in the exercise to the large group.
- Invite participants to comment on films or television shows they have seen that did a good job of depicting these five concepts without a lot of religious language or imagery. At this time, the group members may comment on words other than the one they spent time with.
- Close with the prayer given in the exercise.

CHAPTER 9. PRAYING FOR OTHERS

Intercessory Prayer

At home

- Think about how large your group will be. If you have more than ten people, you might want to break into smaller groups for this prayer. If so, it is important that each group has a leader who keeps the flow of the prayer and includes adequate silence for the imaging.

- You may want to work from a list of prayer requests, which could come from a number of sources (deacons, pastors, the community). If you have some lead time, you could promote the fact that your group will be praying for others and ask for requests.

Introducing the exercise

- It will be important for you to explain beforehand the steps you will be leading participants through. If it helps to give a short handout to the group, then do so.

During the exercise

- You will need to make sure the prayer includes adequate time of silence for the imaging. Keep the flow as follows:
  1. One person begins by stating a prayer request. (They will need to do this aloud in a group. Of course, they may always ask prayers for an unspoken request.) Open the silence with a transition phrase, such as "God be with this person (or situation)."
  2. Allow time in silence for everyone to image God surrounding this person or situation in some way. If there is one large group, you may want to use a chime to end the silence. If you are working in multiple groups and must use the same room, skip the chime.

3. Ask participants to release the person (or situation) fully into God's hands.
4. The leader asks for another request. Repeat steps 1-4 until all requests have been prayed.

After the exercise

- After all requests have been prayed, lead a time of reflection. How did it feel it to pray in this way? Which is more meaningful for you—praying with words or with images? What image of God surrounding a person or situation did you find helpful? Where did you feel the presence of God most actively?
- Close with the "raised arms" prayer stance, as you hand all these prayer concerns over to God.

Healing Prayer

At home

- Spend time considering your beliefs and feelings about healing. Be prepared to lead a discussion about some of our anxieties surrounding healing prayer.

Introducing the exercise

- Explain that we all have seen flashy "faith healers" on television and, for some people, that is what the term "healing prayer" connotes. But this is not flashy prayer, and we do not measure the effectiveness of healing prayer by instantaneous, amazing outcomes. We leave the outcome in God's hands. Our call is to pray and trust.
- Decide before beginning the prayer who or what you will be praying for. If one or more persons has come to the group for healing prayer, you will need to allow time for each one to say a few words about the healing they desire, *but only if they feel comfortable doing so.* If it is a private matter, do not probe.

During the exercise

- You will be the timekeeper. Allow at least five minutes of silence for the time when group members are praying with the light on themselves. Allow ten minutes or more for each prayer request to be surrounded with light.
- You will state the intention as you move through the prayer.
- Move the group to a close after all requests have been considered in prayer.

After the exercise

- Lead a time of reflection on this prayer. What was it like to pray in this way? Have any feelings about healing changed as a result of this prayer? What part of the prayer was easiest for you? What part was hardest? Where was the Spirit most present to you in this prayer?
- Ask the group to consider how healing prayer might gain a more prominent place in the life of an organization (church, spirituality group, hospital)? What keeps people from engaging in healing prayer? What encourages you to pray for healing?
- Close with a prayer, song, or time of silence.

Prayer Partnering

At home

- Decide how long you want the dyads to spend in prayer with one another. The reflection step will take place in the large group.

Introducing the exercise

- Explain the steps of the prayer and the guidelines for "deep listening."
- Explain that this prayer will be done in dyads (pairs). If you have an odd number in your group, the leader will be someone's prayer partner. If there is an even number, the leader will stay on the sidelines as facilitator.
- Advise the dyads to spread out in the room.

During the exercise

- After everyone settles into their dyads, you will start the group off with the prayer given in the exercise.
- Keep an eye on the time. Ring a chime when the dyad time is up, and move participants into a large-group reflection.

After the exercise

- Lead the reflection time, using the questions near the end of the exercise. Listen for any common theme that emerges. Find something in the sharing that moves you.
- Close with a prayer of gratitude, possibly mentioning what moved you in the sharing time.

Franciscan Prayer

At home

- Decide on a group activity that will be the "life situation" for this prayer. For church groups, it could be time in worship or in a committee meeting. For spirituality groups, you could hold a potluck dinner or social event. Make sure you allow time after the activity or event for reflection.

Introducing the exercise

- You will need to explain the prayer and possibly hand out a short list of the steps before the activity or event gets underway.
- Give some background information on Francis of Assisi:
  1. Francis grew up as a wealthy young son of a fabric merchant.
  2. He was a prisoner of war for a year in 1202. Upon returning home, he denounced all wealth and began the life of a beggar and itinerant preacher.
  3. He preached the simple life of joy in Christ.
  4. He embraced and befriended lepers.
  5. Francis developed a huge following without even trying.
  6. His reputation as a lover of animals was based on a legend that he once preached to birds because people were not willing to listen to him.

During the exercise

- Simply be on hand if people have any questions about the exercise. Basically, it's no more than being aware of where you are moved and offering silent, spontaneous prayer in the midst of the activity.

After the exercise

- Lead a time of reflection on the prayer, using the questions listed toward the end of the exercise.
- Close with a circle in which members offer their short, spontaneous Franciscan prayers out loud.

Prayer for the World

At home

- Decide how much time you have and how to divide the various steps of the prayer to accommodate the time.
- Ask participants to bring writing materials with them for this exercise.

Introducing the exercise

- Explain that this exercise is a long, guided meditation that you will lead. It is designed to move us from our particular locations to a concern for the greater world.

During the exercise

- Read the steps slowly and clearly. You will need to allow silence for each step.

After the exercise

- Lead the reflection time, using the questions given at the end of the exercise.
- Lead the closing prayer.

NOTES

2. Basic Contemplative Practices

1. Walter J. Burghardt, "Contemplation—A Long Loving Look at the Real," *Church* (Winter 1989): 14-18.

2. Joan Chittister, *In the Heart of the Temple* (New York: Bluebridge, 2004), 33.

3. Anthony Bloom, *Beginning to Pray* (Mahwah, N.J.: Paulist, 1970), 85-86.

4. Thomas Keating, *Invitation to Love: The Way of Christian Contemplation* (New York: Continuum, 1998), 90.

5. Ibid., see chapter 22, pp. 130-38.

6. Bradley Holt, *Thirsty for God,* 2nd ed. (Minneapolis: Augsburg Fortress, 2005), 80-81.

7. Daniel Wolpert, *Creating a Life with God* (Nashville: Upper Room, 2004), 58.

8. Kallistos Ware, "The Spirituality of the Icon," *The Study of Spirituality* (New York: Oxford Press, 1986), 198.

3. Lectio Divinas

1. M. Basil Pennington, *Lectio Divina* (New York: Crossroad Publishing, 1998), ix.

2. Ibid., 22-23.

3. Martin Luther, "A Simple Way to Pray," in *Luther's Works,* vol. 43, Devotional writings II, trans. Carl J. Schindler, ed. Gustav K. Wiencke (Philadelphia: Fortress, 1968), 187-211.

4. Joseph D. Driskill, *Protestant Spiritual Exercises: Theology, History and Practice* (Harrisburg: Morehouse Publishing, 1999), 93.

5. Saint Francis, "Canticle of the Sun," *The Story of Christian Spirituality,* ed. Gordon Mursell (Minneapolis: Fortress, 2001), 102.

4. Life Reflections

1. Donald St. Louis, "The Ignatian Examen," *The Way of Ignatius Loyola: Contemporary Approaches to the Spiritual Exercises,* Philip Sheldrake, ed. (St. Louis: Institute of Jesuit Sources, 1991), 155.

2. Dennis Linn, Sheila Fabricant Linn, and Matthew Linn, *Sleeping with Bread: Holding What Gives You Life* (Mahwah, N.J.: Paulist, 1995), 5-9.

3. Clyde Crews, *Ultimate Questions: A Theological Primer* (New York: Paulist, 1986), 11.

4. Some questions here adapted from *Seeing God* by Rabbi David Aaron (New York: Tarcher/Putnam, 2001). The "Seeing Exercise" questions are at the end of each chapter.

5. Some of these questions are adapted from *Turning to One Another: Simple Conversations to Restore Hope to the Future,* by Margaret J. Wheatley. (San Francisco: Berrett-Koehler Publishers, 2002).

6. Joseph D. Driskill, *Protestant Spiritual Exercises: Theology, History and Practice* (Harrisburg, Pa.: Morehouse, 1999), 109-13.

7. Barbara Ganim and Susan Fox, *Visual Journaling* (Wheaton, Ill.: Quest, 1999), 17-28.

5. Discernment Processes

1. Wilkie Au, "Holistic Discernment," *Presence: An International Journal of Spiritual Direction* 11, no. 1 (February 2005): 16.

2. Debra K. Farrington, *Hearing with the Heart: A Gentle Guide to Discerning God's Will for Your Life* (San Francisco: Jossey Bass, 2003).

3. David Lonsdale, *Listening to the Music of the Spirit: The Art of Discernment* (Notre Dame, Ind.: Ave Maria Press, 1992), 9.

4. Parker J. Palmer, "The Clearness Committee: A Way of Discernment," *Weavings: A Journal of the Christian Spiritual Life* (July-August 1988): 37-40.

5. *A Dictionary for United Methodists,* ed. Alan K. Waltz (Nashville: Abingdon, 1991), see "Wesleyan Quadrilateral."

6. Body Prayers

1. Stated at a conference at Louisville Theological Seminary, September 1998 and quoted in Kris Haig, "Labyrinth: Christian Spiritual Tool or New Age Gimmick?" *Hungryhearts* (Summer 2000, Vol. 3, No. 2).

2. Marjorie Hoyer Smith, "Embodied Wisdom, Embodied Faith: Bio-Spirituality," *Hungryhearts* 6, no. 3 (Fall/Winter 1997). Reprinted in the

chapter "Praying with our Bodies" in *Lord, Teach Us to Pray: A Guide to Prayer* (published by the Office of Spiritual Formation of the Presbyterian Church USA), 12-15.

3. You can find a wealth of information about the focusing technique and biospirituality at McMahon's Web site at www.biospiritual.org and at the Focusing Institute's Web site, www.focusing.org. A version of Focusing Prayer is described in *Don't Forgive Too Soon* by Dennis Linn, Sheila Fabricant Linn and Matthew Linn (New York: Paulist, 1997), 110-11, and in the self-help book *The Power of Focusing: A Practical Guide to Emotional Self-Healing* by Ann Weiser Cornell (Oakland, Calif.: New Harbinger, 1996). The man credited with researching and designing this technique is retired University of Chicago philosophy professor Eugene T. Gendlin, author of *Focusing* (New York: Everest House, 1978).

4. You can find a finger labyrinth to print on paper at the Web site "Lessons 4 Living," http://www.lessons4living.com/finger_labyrinth.htm. You may even trace the web labyrinth with your mouse pointer to save paper. This site also has a page that shows you how to build your own full-sized labyrinth.

7. Prayers of the Imagination

1. Wolpert's rendition of the "Wall of Prayer" is found in his chapter on writing in a journal, and is written primarily for use with groups. See *Creating a Life with God: The Call of Ancient Prayer Practices* (Nashville: Upper Room, 2004), 111-12.

2. You can find this wonderful story in Gregg Braden, *The Isaiah Effect* (New York: Three Rivers Press, 2000), 160-73.

3. Tanis Helliwell, *Take Your Soul to Work* (Holbrooks, Mass.: Adams Media, 1999), 299-300.

8. Reflections on Media

1. *Lights, Camera, . . . Faith! A Movie Lover's Guide to Scripture,* Peter Malone and Rose Pacatte (Boston: Pauline Books and Media, 2001), 87-91. This is an excellent series of books linking meaningful films with the lectionary passages and liturgical seasons.

9. Praying for Others

1. You can find the original prayer method outlined in Marjorie Thompson, *Soul Feast* (Louisville: Westminster John Knox, 1995) on pages 41-42.

2. Chester P. Michael and Marie C. Norrisey, *Prayer and Temperament: Different Prayer Forms for Different Personality Types* (Charlottesville, Va.: Open Door, 1991), 70. See their chapter on Franciscan prayer on pages 69-78.

3. Joseph Driskill, *Protestant Spiritual Exercises: Theology, History, and Practice* (Harrisburg, Pa.: Morehouse, 1999), 103. The prayer in its entirety is found on pages 102-107.

Leader's Guide

1. Parker J. Palmer. *A Hidden Wholeness: The Journey Toward an Undivided Life* (CITY: Jossey-Bass, 2004), 140.

2. Ibid., 115.